In Their Presence: Best Practices and Stories of Role Models

By

Martin Zimmerman

ISBN: 1-4140-0380-3 (e-book)
ISBN: 1-4140-0379-X (Paperback)
ISBN: 1-4140-0381-1 (Dust Jacket)

Library of Congress Control Number: 2003096702

This book is printed on acid free paper.

Printed in the United States of America
Bloomington, IN

1stBooks - rev. 10/21/03

This book is dedicated to my loving wife, Luanne, and to my two daughters, Ingrid and Siri, who create such an abundance of joy and energy in my life.

This book is also dedicated to every human being on this Earth, in our collective quest for meaning and making a difference.

Acknowledgements

I wish to thank the people with whom I shared the feedback, many of whom encouraged me to write a book on feedback meetings we experienced together. My friends and former neighbors, Kate and Dave Bridge, always suggested I write this book. Later, I presented this subject for thirty minutes to the Rotary Club of Davisburg, Michigan, whose members, from ages thirty to ninety-eight, provided a warm reception and encouraged me to write this book.

Appreciation goes to Priscilla Thate and to my wife Luanne, who proofread my manuscript and improved its readability. Thanks to Karen Smith, the editor for the Clarkston Eccentric newspaper. While working to go on vacation and volunteering community service time, she gladly squeezed in a couple of hours to answer my questions and provided advice and encouragement.

Finally, thanks to all the people who took the time from their busy life schedules to read my unedited manuscript and provide insights to encourage you, the reader, to invest your time in discovering the treasures within this book.

More Endorsements for
In Their Presence: Best Practices and Stories of Role Models

"This book provides authentic insight into the possibilities of being a true role model. Rarely do we have the opportunity to tap into the feedback conversations of over 1,600 leaders, much less in such an informative way. This book will be invaluable for those who aspire to be leaders or for those who have held a leadership title for a long time. This is definitely going on my recommended reading list!"

Marsha Clark, Marsha Clark & Associates

"I was fortunate to witness the first presentation Marty made sharing what would become the contents of this book. Utilizing this collection of materials, Marty is an excellent inspirational speaker whom I would recommend to any organization. The insights shared in this book are of great use to business leaders, community leaders and service clubs alike."

Gerald Jackson, Assistant District Governor, Rotary International District 6380

"Never before in the history of business has the need for sound, competent and authentic role models been so critical. One has only to read the newspapers to see that something has gone wrong with respect to the integrity of our business leaders. Marty's experience in measuring, interviewing and delivering feedback to leaders provides valuable insight into behaviors that work and lead organizations to success."

Prudence Cole, President & CEO, being@work

"Marty Zimmerman captures the essences of exemplary leadership...*In Their Presence: Best Practices and Stories of Role Models*. He gives dynamic examples of real-life business practice that spell real leadership! This gives the reader at all levels genuine examples to act and live by. I am impressed."
Mack Gaston, Rear Admiral, USN, (Ret.)

"Why does leadership in our day, and in all areas of life, appear to be in crisis? Many have responded to that question in different ways. Marty Zimmerman brings fresh insights to the question and helps us look into areas that we might least expect to find an answer. He comes to those insights through years of careful analysis of case studies and experience with leadership development and shares them with us in this exciting piece of work. A must-read book for anyone who aspires to be a leader."
Monsignor Robert S. Humitz, Pastor, St. Daniel Community, Clarkston, Michigan; author *Reliving the Glory*

"This book reflects the comments I heard from participants regarding Marty and their personal development. I had the privilege of being Marty's leader and I know the passion and professionalism he carried into every feedback session. This book also reflects Marty's ability to listen—with his ears, with his eyes, with his very being—and his ability to connect with people. A quote attributed to Decouvertes says, 'It is not the answer that enlightens, but the question.' Marty was always excellent at asking the right questions and this book is a result of many right questions."
Ron Holleman

Table of Contents

Preface xi

Chapter 1:   Motivation.. 1

Chapter 2:   Strategic or Visionary Thinking 29

Chapter 3:   Risk Taking/Decisiveness.......................... 53

Chapter 4:   Business 67

Chapter 5:   Negotiations and Resolving Conflict........ 79

Chapter 6:   Client Focused 93

Chapter 7:   People Care—Coaching, Team Orientation,
                Communicating and Sharing the Knowledge 97

Chapter 8:   Integrity and Convictions 125

Chapter 9:   Leadership.. 143

Chapter 10:   Conclusion 157

Appendix   Sample Comments and Questions from Role
                Models 159

References.. 167

x

Preface

Purpose

Who is this book for?

This book, while business is its context, is for readers of all ages and one profession, the profession of life. Just as role models profess to what they say or do, we, likewise, reflect our own profession in word and deed. The stories and thoughts from role models within these pages are all about life.

This book is for those who aspire to be the best that they can be. I believe that if you want to become the best, study the practices of the best.

This book is for those passionate about living in, and being a part of, the collective wisdom of human beings. This wisdom is reflected through the stories and comments within these pages. The deep thinker in us realizes it is more than simply a matter of mimicking the actions and words of these role models. It requires appreciating their universal philosophies, values and attitudes that form the basis for their observable habits of outward expression. Taking what others model for us and adapting that to our style and environment helps us to realize our human spirit. We learn more about ourselves.

This book is for the curiosity within us, to compare the things that we do with what others are doing. Willingness to take a risk and chart a change in our behavior and thinking is our choice. We can choose that which helps make a difference to our life's journey, seeking and creating meaning.

Granted, you will be at some disadvantage compared to the participant leaders. The participants had a perspective of seeing their documented feedback from people who know them well. We typically do not get to see such a tangible view of what is often intangible, yet powerful. We do not get to see such a measured and visual view of the perceptions of others across performance behaviors. This book serves to counter that disadvantage for you. You get to see yourself in any of the brief stories I share about myself and those of the role models. You get to see yourself by responding to reflective questions. I invite you to take a challenge while you read this book. It's the challenge of introspection and reflecting personally and frankly with one's self. As an employee, and as a person outside of work, think about how you behave. The behaviors described by the role models within are transferable. You can readily transfer the workplace examples for role model practices into other domains of your life outside work. These apply in both a formal and informal leadership capacity. These behaviors apply to school, church, athletics, family, business or any life domain where service and relationship to others is key. Think about the everyday pattern of behaviors collected from role model participant leaders within. Look for what you can leverage. It is **yours** for the taking.

As you discover the messages in these pages, questions like the following will provide a catalyst for further thinking and practice. How do you compare what you do to their responses? Do you see yourself frequently behaving in ways similar to how the role models describe their habits? How about every once in a while? Or not at all? What does that suggest to you? Questions like these will serve to marinate your discovery process. It is one thing to see the common messages of the role models in print. It transfers into added personal value to simulate the experience of being in their presence. These pages will serve that end and also help you identify the role models in your own life.

The aim here is not to imply that simply reading this book and duplicating these behaviors makes you a role model. However, I believe there is role model potential still waiting to be developed in us all, notwithstanding our past accomplishments. This work is not designed to close the book on what role models do. Rather than close down the inquiry, this book is designed to open and continue the inquiry.

The aim is not to become superhuman. Even the role model leaders I met were role models for some of the behaviors, not all of the behaviors in the executive and leadership feedback surveys.

The aim is to increase your adaptability and capacity to take action and achieve results. Like the role models, you can aspire to seek continued meaning in your life. You can awaken that dormant internal potential beckoning to enrich your life even more.

In the last chapter, Leadership, I refer to one way of defining leadership as the ability to connect with another human being. If you are in the business of truly connecting with other human beings, then you are in the business of what this book has to offer.

My challenge to you—I invite you to take this journey. Try even one of the suggestions to which you most relate from the many stories within for a month, each day. After thirty days, ask yourself, "What difference do I notice from the verbal feedback of others?" It will be worth more than the cost of this book and your time to read it. Thank you for the time you invested in reading this book. Share it with those for whom you care. Enjoy!

- Marty

Background

I have interviewed business leaders known to be role models for particular leadership behaviors, based on reliable measurement. Repeatedly, I heard a definitive pattern of similar responses to a question such as the following: "What do you think you do or say that causes all your respondents to indicate a high frequency for motivation in the workplace?"

For five years, I served the role of a multi-rater feedback coach for a global corporation. I met, individually, with over 1,600 leaders, from supervisory through the executive level. This diverse group of leaders included male and female, with educational levels from high school graduate through doctorate. This represents a broad spectrum of personal backgrounds and varying work environments. This company's philosophy required locating many of their leaders with their clients. This resulted in interviewing leaders in diverse work environments. These ranged from office spaces to the louder and larger plant and warehousing settings. The industries included financial, energy, retail, transportation, manufacturing, health, government, insurance, banking, communications and more.

The business people assessing the participant leader are called respondents. These respondents knew and associated with the leader on a regular basis. They included one or more of the participant leader's own leaders. Also represented were the participant leader's clients and peers and the employees who worked for that participant leader. The leader who requested the feedback from his respondents we'll call the participant leader, or participant. This is the basis for referring to this form of feedback as multi-rater feedback.

The process of providing feedback required me to present the written, numerical feedback results to the requesting participant leader being assessed. This occurred in a two to three-hour, confidential, one-on-one meeting. Confidentiality of our meeting meant that I could not identify a specific respondent's feedback to the participant leader. These respondents knew that their feedback was confidential. Confidentiality also meant I could not identify a specific participant leader's feedback by name. As a result, I will only refer to comments made by participant leaders in this book as coming from a participant. They are not identified by name.

Participant comments enclosed in quotation marks represent their ideas regarding how they demonstrate specific behaviors and do not represent a word for word, or literal, response.

A standard frequency scale guided respondents submitting feedback. They used this scale to rate how often they observed that leader demonstrating each behavior. The scale included a *not applicable* or *not observed* option. It gradually increased in frequency from less than 25 percent of the time on the lower end. The mid range was marked by 50 percent of the time. At the highest end was 100 percent frequency and role model. This frequency scale forms the basis for what I refer to as participant leaders achieving role model ratings in this book. I asked the following question of participant leaders who received very high ratings, or role model ratings: "What do you think you do or say to cause all your respondents to mark you 'always' (100 percent frequency), or even mark you a 'role model' for this behavior?" The similarity of responses from such a diverse, internationally dispersed group of participant leaders working in different environments inspired me to share my story with you.

As a performance feedback coach, I was in a unique position to observe when various participant leaders had requested feedback from some of the same respondents. The respondents who marked role model markings for one participant leader were marking another not even 50 percent of the time for the same behavior(s). I realized these same respondents were using the entire spectrum of the frequency scale. They were mindfully completing these feedback surveys on their leader(s). I concluded that respondents marked behaviors in a good faith effort that reflected a judicious, conscientious intent. This further validated the results for me. So when role models spoke, I listened. I share their insights, practices and wisdom with you here.

As an unbiased third party, my role as a feedback coach was as the participants' tour guide, not as their judge or psychologist. I took them on a tour of their data and helped them to understand their feedback, as an unbiased third party. We identified and appreciated their strengths as well as their developmental areas. Our conversation prompted their thinking about kinds of behavioral changes they could see themselves making, and for what purpose.

Chapters 1-9 present some of the major areas of leadership performance behaviors evaluated and measured. These chapters introduce key sets of behaviors and tie the specific patterns of comments from the high-scoring participant leaders. I refer to these high-scoring participant leaders as role model leaders within this book. I was struck by the similarity of responses given by role model leaders for specific behaviors. These behaviors are considered critical to leadership effectiveness. Not exhibiting these behaviors usually resulted in relationship breakdowns and lower overall effectiveness and productivity. This degraded their potential to achieve business success.

1

Motivation

To my question: "How do you live such a long life?"
His immediate reply: "Just don't think about it."
                                                    —Clarence Aspenson

What persuades me to choose motivation as the first chapter?

Behavior statements about motivation and inspiration referred to asking respondents how frequently did the participant inspire people to excel and to care about their work. Also, how frequently did they motivate others, even others not in constant contact with them?

When I began providing feedback to participants in my role as a performance feedback coach, I did not anticipate hearing similar responses from diverse role model participants. It was the repetitive messages in the responses of role model participants to the question, "What do you think you do or say that causes all your respondents to mark so highly?" The commonality of their responses initially surfaced to me in the area of motivation. This first made me aware of common, repetitive practices among different leaders in different environments and in different parts of the world across the range of leadership behaviors.

One hallmark of a great feedback coach is the ability to ask the question in a way that encourages a person to more deeply access the insight from within. It is asking the question that draws forth that wisdom of human understanding and insight within each of us. One of the role model participants for motivation was a linguist by education. She spoke several languages fluently. As she reflected on what she typically did or said to create such a high perception of motivation, she told me, "Marty, the word 'life' and the word 'motivation' come from the same root word."

With that insight, I would often ask an additional question to help the participants think about how their data for motivation reflected their verbal and nonverbal practices. To the question, "In conversation or association with you, what's your sense of people walking away? Are they more often feeling life, energy, motivation? Or, leaving your presence, do they more often feel de-life, something other than life, less motivation?" As a feedback coach, I experienced participants responding more deeply and comprehensively to this question. As opposed to simply translating the behavior statement into a question such as, "What do you think you say or do that causes people to say you motivate them?"

What follows are four major patterns or responses that I heard from the role models for motivation and inspiration in the workplace. Included is an assortment of supporting comments and stories from these participants while they were reflecting on their numerical feedback.

(1) *Positive over negative*

The power and advantage of focusing on the positive and not dwelling on the negative is the first major pattern of response, as captured by some of the following comments from role models.

"Marty, the bottle is half full, not half empty."

"I'll ask them, 'What was **good** about the customer yelling at us this morning?'"

"While these issues remain, where have we come from? What progress have we made?"

"Can do, not can't do, is in my vocabulary. You can test others' outlook by how often you either hear them essentially say 'can do,' or 'can't do.'"

"When I'm validating or confirming, I'm being positive. If I notice a habit of second guessing in mine or others' language, that's a sign of negative, bottle is half empty." (This participant also tied this to demonstrating confident decisiveness.)

"When I feel down, say my client just yelled at me and directed that we cut costs more, I still maintain a positive demeanor with the next person I see. My problem isn't going to help my people get their job done. The next person I meet is one of my people who just worked all weekend and it's now Monday morning. I still vigorously thank them. And I continue thinking of alternative opportunities to seek new business. It's nothing personal with that client."

"I have learned that when I appear self-absorbed, I give the appearance as less positive, as opposed to engaging outwardly."

"It's important to be nice and courteous to yourself. Loosen up internally by being willing to give yourself the benefit of the doubt. Remember the good in what you did in a situation you self-analyze."

"I exclude, or only involve at a minimum, the cynics. Cynics just slow you down."

"No matter when, even if I'm down, to the question, 'How are you?' I respond, 'Never been better,' or I respond, 'Great.' Even when I'm having a bad day."

"I coach others to change their focus from what they cannot control to what they can control, which promotes a positive orientation and a higher level of excellence."

"I'll say things like, 'Let's step back—there's some positive here—we sold two contracts this month. Yes, we didn't get three others, that's for another day. This is a marathon, not a sprint. Pace yourself to get through to the end.'"

"I have a positive attitude and people hear me say things like, 'We'll get through this.'"

"I promote thinking positive, smiling and not dwelling on the negative, on what we cannot control. I share humor."

How often do you dwell on the negative? As I see it, the operative word here is the word "dwell." It is not that one overlooks what is negative or avoids considering it. Have you ever been told that you dwell on the negative? This last participant's comment hits home. I can relate to dwelling on the negative. Recalling those situations in my lifetime where dwelling on what went wrong, and how bad things appeared, it strikes me that the dwelling only produced a sense of hopelessness and usually made matters predictably worse. The specifics to those situations varied, but the feelings of frustration, anger, hopelessness and futile despair did not vary. Dwelling on what we cannot control leads to a tendency to manipulate and not connect with human beings. I probably owe a wrinkle or two on the brow from camping out on the negatives in life. In the words of Dr. Martin Luther King, "Free at last. Free at last. Thank God Almighty. Free at last!"

As you continue reading, notice how the comments of other role model leaders indicate a similar theme throughout this book.

They are sounding off on the same message from different perspectives.

(2) *Fun*

"Life is not so serious, Marty, that we can't have fun along the way."

"Icebreakers at a team meeting, or the use of humor, as long as it's appropriate, make our tough environment bearable and relaxes a lot of tension."

"The ability to laugh at ourselves is one of our biggest strengths."

"Having fun relaxes the tension around here and frees up people's creativity."

"I laugh at least once a day, to include laughing at myself."

"A sample icebreaker is for each person to tell two truths and one fib about themselves, and the others guess the fib."

"Humor downplays the negative aspects and promotes the good. Our world tends to orchestrate bad news in the communication waves, so be selective."

"I saw a study indicating that an optimistic view and attitude will promote a life span seven years longer. I personally believe in that power of positive thinking."

"When positive and happy, I notice people are focused on solutions. When negative and unhappy, they're focused on complaining."

On this note of fun, I visited one role model leader whose office was, unfortunately, located at the darkened end of a narrow corridor. However, he turned his misfortune into fortune and capitalized on the drawback. He featured a physical example of what led to a highly motivating environment. He auspiciously posted signs greeting you as you approached his door, such as "Dead End," and, "Enter at Your Own Risk." They turned a cool, uninviting physical environment into one more inviting and warm. Indeed, people apparently preferred meeting at his office.

(3) *Nonverbal*

The participants do not use the word "nonverbal." Its use here describes these following two major subsets of responses.

(a) *Smile versus frown*

"I've been told I wear a smile on my face."

"Marty, I had received feedback that made me realize when I frown, people are thinking I disapprove or that I'm bothered or displeased. It's precisely when I'm interested, when I'm deep in thought about something, that I'm frowning."

This particular leader determined he was sending mixed messages between his verbal and nonverbal expressions. His example follows.

"I tell new employees to come to me with their ideas. That is a reason for hiring them. What happens when a new employee comes to me with an idea, a new proposal, and my normal, nonverbal response as I initially think about it is to automatically frown? What first impression do you think that new employee is receiving? What's the chance they'll want to bring me more good ideas? So one thing I have learned to consciously say is something like—'What you're proposing here really intrigues me.' Or I'll say, 'I want you to know I'm frowning now because I'm deep in thought.'"

Notice an important distinction as stated by the latter participant. When this leader decided to make a behavior change, he chose to do something that was natural for him. Instead of focusing on trying to intentionally smile or stop frowning, when he received a new idea, he rather developed a habit of consciously adding a statement ("This really intrigues me") that communicated the intent of his nonverbal response. Others could now more accurately read or interpret the intentions behind his nonverbal expressions.

(b) *Sitting next to someone versus standing over them*

"Marty, when I walk around and talk with people at their place, I always pull up a chair and sit next to them all the time."

First, a story that presents one of my more dramatic experiences as a feedback coach. For the motivation behavior, of over 1,600 total leaders that I met, only three of them had received role model markings from all their respondents for that behavior. I asked each of them, "What do you think you do or say that causes everyone to mark you 'role model?'" Each of them gave the same initial response, which was sitting next to people when they visit as opposed to standing over them.

Each of these three leaders offered additional responses for what they thought they routinely did to create such a high pattern of perception for motivation. Significant to me, though, was that each of these three people gave the same initial response. They did not know each other, were in totally different geographic locations and work environments, and had not attended the same class on motivating employees! I was especially keen to ensure that I did not inadvertently influence them into responding the same by how I asked the question. Was this just coincidence? I chalked the first two role models' initial responses as just coincidental. I had met them separately over the course of a year and did not think I would ever again encounter a participant with all role model ratings for the motivation behavior. While the first two were men leading in strictly white-collar office environments, the third, a woman, led in a manufacturing, blue-collar environment.

When I asked her what she said or did, she replied, "I'm out there with my people all the time."

To which I replied, "If I were to pass by and see you out there with your people, how would you appear to me?"

Her response, "I'd be sitting next to them. Is that what you mean?"

Later, I shared feedback with a leader who also taught statistics as a professor at a major university. He told me, in so many words, that if they each gave the same initial response under the circumstances as I described them, then there was something statistical about that.

Prior to this experience, if you had asked me for fifty examples of motivation, I do not believe I would have offered sitting next to people as one of those fifty examples.

More on sitting next to people one on one

One of the role model leaders for motivation commented, "Marty, when I stand there over my employees, talking to them, I'm subliminally reinforcing command and control and hierarchy. As soon as I pull up a chair and sit next to them, conversation is different, just like that."

Sometimes, certain behaviors will correlate, or relate more closely to each other, such that similar actions may produce consistent results in feedback for multiple behaviors. One leader's data was somewhat lower for both the motivation behavior and the behavior 'respects others.' This leader was a large-sized individual. He expressed surprise that the behavior for respect was low, because he was not aware of any obvious signs of showing disrespect. However, he became more aware of the cause for this low perception in frequency as we discussed possibilities. One of them was his habit of sitting or leaning on employees' desks as he talked with them. I asked him what might people be thinking about that? He hypothesized that they could be thinking, "How rude. You're in my space, parking yourself on my desktop." His reasoning for doing so was to create less of a formality. He was discovering that the message conveyed to others was different from what he intended.

Can you relate to this? Have you done some things with good intention, unaware of the actual message being received?

This story had a good ending. The leader determined adjustments he could make, to walk the talk of respect more clearly. He later confirmed with his employees, in a spirit of openness, that, indeed, what he had hypothesized during our meeting had been their thinking. This illustrates a change in behavior one person made by remaining open to what others were indicating. The constructive results this person gleaned from their numerical data and written feedback comments corroborated their conclusions and fueled his resolve to change.

Time

There are those of us who could be thinking—sounds good Marty, but I don't have the time to pull up a chair and sit next to people. It's more efficient to talk on the fly. This presents a legitimate concern. After all, the information age requires speed, accelerated information flow and more.

First, one need not take one specific habit that role models claim they follow and do them 100 percent of the time. Sitting next to people as a habit does not exclude standing and talking to people on occasion. The real message here is whether our habit of communicating with people precludes connecting with others in a way that promotes life and energy.

Second, this refers back to one of those three leaders mentioned earlier with a complete role model rating from all their respondents. I asked her if her client, a manufacturing plant manager who was one of the respondents to her feedback, ever noticed her sitting with her people. She replied, "Yes." That suggests to me that a person such as the plant manager, in a position that, by reputation and necessity, sees efficiency as a premium in the workplace, somehow also saw her sitting next to her people as a contributing factor to her being a motivational role model.

Third, one leader put it this way: "Marty, I don't park next to them when I sit down beside them. I may only sit there for thirty seconds and say something like, 'Still good to go from our conversation yesterday? Good. You know where I'm at otherwise, should you need me?' And off I go with the chair."

Is it really elementary too?

During a feedback meeting, one of the participants, upon hearing the idea of sitting next to people, had a reaction. Her face suddenly shone, as if having what I call a life-bulb thought. Invited to speak to some second-grade classes years previous, she recalled receiving a phone call from the school principal afterward.

This veteran principal of many years generally made it a habit to stop in and listen whenever guest speakers presented, both as a courtesy and as an interested party. Besides thanking the participant, the principal offered to her that in all her years of observing guest speakers, she realized this particular presentation had left an especially invigorating impact on the students. The principal's conclusion was that this participant, unlike previous speakers, did not remain at the head of the room. Instead, this speaker casually moved to various locations among the class, sitting and talking in one area of students, then effortlessly proceeding to move and sit through the rest of the class audience.

What registered for me, at the moment of hearing that story, was a realization that our children feel the energy and a sense of enthusiasm from adults who get down to their level. I suddenly saw ourselves as adults in the business world, extensions of the children we once were. What was brought home to me was the universality of this work for all of us. Does what inspires us today as adults inspire us similarly as children?

Indication of immediate impact

I stumbled onto some dramatic evidence of the power of sitting next to people compared to the opposite behavior of standing over them when conversing. I had occasion to share feedback with a leader in a location on a Monday. I shared with him the behavior of sitting next to people. On Wednesday, I returned to that same building to share feedback with yet another leader. Again, I found it appropriate to share that same sitting next to people behavior with this participant as we discussed motivation. I had not even finished offering the insight, when she suddenly began rocking in her chair and repeatedly said, "I know that works. I know that works."

I asked her, "How do you know that works?"

Her reply, "My boss sat beside me for the first time yesterday."

"Really?"

"Yes, and you know what?"

"What?"

"For the first time, I felt like he was genuinely listening to me and not just pretending."

While careful to ensure confidentiality, I asked her the name of her leader. The answer she gave me was the name of the person I had talked to on Monday. He was a manager with an office and she was one of his supervisors, who worked out of what they call a double cube space in the cube aisle areas. (These cubes were partitions of varying height bordering a person's desk, designed to give employees some privacy.)

It is a rare opportunity for me to catch such an immediate impression from a person on the receiving end of a change in a participant's behavior directly due to one of our feedback meetings, as had occurred at this time. Yet this cause and effect glimpse of one person's change in behavior and the direct affect his behavior change had on another reveals actual reality, not theory and supposition.

One of Oprah Winfrey's shows featured a theme that when people showed a kindness to a stranger, that kindness tended to be passed on to yet another. While one of the examples was a person paying the toll for the car behind them at the tollbooth, this kindness

11

can be in the form of human currency far exceeding any nation's monetary currency.

This also proclaims some good news—that one primary change in one person's behavior potentially has a multiplying, ripple effect. In this example, the impact went beyond a feeling of increased energy to include an increased ability to communicate. And you can bet the manager noted above did not take a communication class on Monday night or Tuesday morning in order to display his increased ability to communicate and listen as perceived by the receiver, the supervisor working for this manager. Just think from a leader's perspective; one change in behavior has the ability to affect multiple people. What's more, unless we are restricted to an isolation room, all of us, no matter our position in the formal hierarchical organization chart, have the ability to affect multiple people daily.

Some people might call this a synergistic effect. I call it the power we each have to influence, in a world we cannot control, and leave our mark!

A possibility

A participant told me about some research he recalled. Whatever the intent of the research, the participant maintained that the researchers were surprised by what they concluded. That is, that when one or more people were standing, a conversation typically took on a more stressful quality than when all people were seated. They observed that this occurred independently of age, gender and locality. Their conclusion was that this was rooted in our ancestral programming. When we were standing upright, we tended to be more on guard, ready for some sudden threat, such as the spring of the tiger. When we were seated, we were more relaxed and let down our guard.

I have no proof beyond hearsay that such research existed, or precisely what it studied or its conclusions. However, just consider the notion that the quality of our conversations today, and the behavior of sitting next to people as one of the patterns cited by role model leaders for motivation, could be influenced by habits developed thousands of years ago. That presents an intriguing thought.

Team orientation and sitting next to people

During one feedback meeting, a participant rated a role model for both motivation and for promoting a team orientation shared this story.

As this leader and I explored her feedback, we had already talked about her high marks for motivation. Later in the feedback meeting, I asked her what she did or said to make her a role model for the team-oriented category of behaviors. These behaviors include developing mutual accountability among team members; promoting productive cooperation between groups; delegating; leveraging an assortment of skills and styles of diverse work teams to achieve results; and publicly rewarding the team. At one point, she requested we take a break and she would show me.

She walked me through the aisles housing her employees. Instead of the traditional, corporate mandated cubes, the aisles were wide open. Each person had a privacy partition on just one side, instead of three sides of the desktop. Each aisle was open to itself and a round table with an extra chair was placed on both sides of the open aisle. This promoted impromptu meetings and problem-solving discussions. I noted how the employees appeared upbeat, smiling, and you could both see and hear the energy among them.

As if the ghost of Christmas Past, she beckoned, "Follow me," as she led me to the other side of the floor. Here existed the traditional cube structure, with every person seated at their desk, within their box-like partition. You could hear an occasional cough or low voice. It was as if you could hear a pin drop, as the saying goes.

Back in her office, she explained that the quiet area belonged to her peer's team of employees. Her own team had also been formerly housed in that same standard cube environment mandated by her corporate organization. The team decided it needed to open up the physical environment to promote the collaborative approach to working they determined necessary to be more productive and to achieve their business goals. It took the leader much time and patience with both her corporate organization and corporate real estate to change the rules. Once accomplished, she had data to support the obvious increase in morale and energy of the team. That data now also included the results of her multi-rater feedback, exceeding the averages of her peers.

I will always remember the dramatic difference between the two groups, partly influenced by the physical layout itself. This more open layout enabled all team members to sit beside one another in even brief conversations.

Now, on to the fourth major factor role model leaders cited for being seen so frequently as motivating.

(4) *Verbally thanking others*

A fourth pattern of response from role model leaders for motivation is, as one participant leader put it, "**Verbally thanking others for little things all the time**." The examples given by participants did not infer inflating remarks, expressing thanks just for the sake of expressing thanks, nor expressing thanks for what employees are minimally expected to do (thanks for coming to work on time today). Rather, their examples characterized timely, brief, specific and pointed feedback.

> ✳ "Yeah, Marty. Walking out of a team meeting with another, I'll say to them, 'I, for one, appreciate your biting your tongue in there for the last half-hour, and I know practicing patience is tough for you. But I think we all benefited from hearing the customer being able to vent.'"

> ✳ "Well, just this morning, as I passed by, seeing one of my team members in the hallway for the first time today, I said, 'Thanks for your voice mail message yesterday. It got me thinking about this in a way I had never thought of before. Really appreciate it.'"

Both verbal appreciation and verbal acknowledgement were mentioned together by the role models. The words they expressed acknowledged the value or contribution people made in little ways over time, without necessarily always saying the actual words "Thank you" or "I appreciate that."

Some of these participants also noted a habit of writing thank you notes and cards or encouraging the client to write thank you notes recognizing that leader's employees, whenever appropriate.

However, the preponderance of responses I heard from these role models for attributing what they always do or say to create a high perception of motivation centered around expressing verbal, on the spot appreciation or acknowledgement to their stakeholders. Many did not even consciously seem to be aware of how much they did this, until they had their data staring so strongly at them in our meeting. Notice, too, just from a couple of their examples, that offering verbal appreciation was a part of their normal conversational talk with people. For them, giving verbal appreciation or acknowledgement was not a big deal. Yet for those on the receiving end, it appeared to be a big deal. People felt more life, energy and motivation in association with people expressing these habits.

Do you enjoy moments of instant gratification? Could you verbally provide more of those moments for both yourself and others?

Upon finishing the paragraphs above, I stopped writing to drive a family friend, Rosemary, to her doctor's appointment. While remaining in the waiting area after she was called in to see the doctor, I was struck by the busyness of the doctor's office. Shortly before Rosemary returned, the doctor poked her head into the lobby, looked at me and said, "Thank you for bringing Rosemary to her appointment. That is so nice of you." Imagine my surprise. How rare it would be for doctors today, with so much on their minds, to think to do what this doctor demonstrated that day. And, again, is it coincidence, or more, that I had just completed this section on verbal appreciation? I felt those very feelings of life and energy on the receiving end of that brief exchange with the good doctor.

When was the last time you offered a verbal thank you or verbally acknowledged another's deeds? Did it occur in the last conversation you had with another person—be it a co-worker, client, spouse, child, neighbor, even a stranger? If it did, that, too, may be more than coincidence!

Oprah Winfrey idea

Towards the conclusion of each feedback meeting, we devoted some time to developmental next steps. Here we would discuss, and I would listen to the participant's desire to change some behavior(s). I was always careful in my own mind to ensure that people were making changes that were compatible with who they were, their values and their beliefs. A desire to more often verbally express thanks is just such an example. I occasionally heard a participant say that verbally thanking people was not a cultural habit of theirs. One person, of Norwegian background, stated that among some Norwegians, if you did not hear something, then everything was fine. If there were a problem, then you would hear about it! (I married into a Norwegian family, so I know!)

When I received feedback on myself as a participant, I realized that thanking people often was something I happened to do, without much thought to doing it. This was a case where, if it was easy for me, I certainly did not want to presume it was easy, or appropriate, for just anyone else. I also felt that for this to become a life-changing behavior, one that took root, instead of becoming a temporary phenomena, required more than just setting a goal to say thank you three or thirty times a day for, say, thirty days. Then, a chance event occurred that gave me an idea.

My wife would video record a daily morning television show featuring Regis Philbin on the ABC network in the United States. For years we enjoyed *Live with Regis and Kathie Lee*, and then *Live with Regis and Kelly*. This became our evening entertainment. The benefits of a VCR include fast forwarding through commercials and repeats. Then, one day a few years ago, my wife decided to tape the last minutes of an *Oprah Winfrey* show. She thought I might find the topic on the show to be of special interest. Indeed I did.

What I most recall about that show was Oprah referring to having written down approximately five things she was thankful for in a journal at the end of each day for a length of time. Paraphrasing what I recall Oprah saying, she basically looked into the camera and said, "I plead with you, please consider writing down five things you are thankful for at the end of each day. No other thing has most impacted my life as has doing this. It will change your life as it has changed mine."

Taking that offer from Oprah and running with it, I have suggested precisely doing just that as a development activity for participants wanting to increase verbally thanking others as part of their normal behavior. In other words, it may take more than to just scratch the surface developmentally. It may take more than setting a goal that says I will verbally thank people five times each day in the workplace. That alone may lead to discovering at five minutes until the end of a shift that I still have five minutes left to thank people five times! In essence, real change may better occur by writing down five things you are thankful for at the end of each day for a month. At the end of that month, notice what changes have occurred. For example, see if you have heard any feedback from others around you signifying some change in you.

Have you noticed yourself more consciously thinking about and offering some verbal feedback as it occurs to you during the day?

Reading through your list of five reasons each day for a month, what stands out to you?

Do you see the positives in things more? Does that occur more naturally to you than before?

Do mental observations in your life of what is wonderful or appreciated take on more clarity and awareness as you document those occasions?

Are you now aware of something in life not previously known to you?

What change, if any, have you noticed after a month of good faith effort writing five things you are thankful for at the conclusion of each day?

How has it changed your perspective, your life, as Oprah suggests?

There's yet more

When wrapping up the page of behaviors on Inspiration, which included the motivation behavior, I would ask the participants who showed role model markings for this entire section this question: "Before we turn this page to the next set of behaviors, is there anything else, beyond what you have already stated at the specific behavior level, that you think causes all your respondents to say 'always' and 'role model' for all the behaviors on this page of Inspiration?" I would usually hear one of four responses—"Nothing more to say," "Chocolates," "Color," or "Both chocolates and color."

Chocolates

Participant leaders would have a bowl or basket of chocolates available in their office, or at their place, for people to enjoy. I particularly noticed in the U.S. a trend toward Hershey's miniatures, Reese's miniature peanut butter cups and M&Ms. However, other countries had delicious chocolates as well. In Ottawa, for example, I was treated during one feedback meeting to some phenomenal sampling of special, dark, Canadian chocolate.

As one leader put it, "Marty, the more chocolate they eat, the more they talk. More ideas, more productivity." (After all, this is a business setting with a business motive here!)

Another leader specified, "Chocolate attracts people like honey does bees."

Leaders often had other treats available, such as pretzels, hard candies and mints. But chocolate ruled the day.

One leader, upon hearing about the chocolate, proudly pointed up to his chocolate. It was in a sealed crystal jar, setting on top of the highest cabinet, furthest from the door in his office. He immediately caught himself and proceeded to reach for it, unsealed the lid and placed it near the doorway. I asked him, in case the chocolate held some special significance, did he want to do that? He claimed no sentimental attachment. As he lowered the crystal jar and took off the top, it physically appeared as if he was letting go of some load from his shoulders. He began to clarify other things he had been remiss in

18

doing that he could associate to the lower frequency of data for some of the behavior statements throughout his feedback survey.

Color

This refers to the displaying of color or a combination of color and conversation items at their workspace. Role model leaders attributed a preponderance of color and conversation pieces prominently featured at their workplace as another factor influencing people's perception of being inspirational. While picture frames of family are important conversation pieces, this goes beyond the pictures to include evidence of hobbies, artistic preferences and evidence of favorite vacation spots. This assortment of colorful decorations and memorabilia mirrored the leader's culture, history, life beyond work and personal tastes. It made it easier for employees to get to know their leader.

When meeting a leader for a feedback meeting at their place, I had an advantage to get a first impression view, similar to that of a new employee's first day on the job. Since I met over 1,600 leaders in five years, that meant I observed over 1,600 offices or places these leaders physically occupied. I could then relate what I observed, first impression, along with the feedback the leader was receiving. Sometimes, I would ask the leader if I could share my first impressions. In this case, when leaders desired thought starters to understand how they were perceived infrequently as inspirational, I might invite them to look around their relatively barren offices. I asked them, "If you were a new employee coming in here and saw the stacks of work and lack of informal conversation pieces, what nonverbal messages might you be seeing?" Their answers showed how obvious it became to them.

"All work and no play."

"So much for my job security, my leader could be moved out in five minutes!"

"It's OK to talk about work, but anything else
is a waste of my valuable time."

These comments came from the self-reflections of leaders possessing relatively barren offices and workspaces—barren of warmth, of anything other than who I am as a fellow employee.

According to the role models, the mere presence of color, of life beyond work, of art, translates to building trust and to a heightened level of employee commitment and innovation. The trends of statistical feedback data punctuated these lessons like exclamation points. The claim here is not that color and conversation pieces alone ensure the building of trust and innovation. The lesson is that, in conjunction with a spirit and desire to connect with others, these serve to definitely contribute to fostering these real, albeit intangible, leadership traits.

Does this mean one only needs to buy a bag of chocolates and hang personal conversation starters in one's office to be inspirational? There is a deeper message here.

I recall entering one participant's office, seeing the stuffed animals, some waterfalls, figurines, colorful plants, chocolates and her unit's strategic business plan posted like a border below the ceiling. Sure enough, she was a role model for both inspiration and as one promoting strategic, visionary thinking.

One participant noted with pride that he noticed people could walk into his office whenever the door was open, take some chocolate from the bowl and leave without feeling obliged to ask for permission. To him, their not having to seek permission each time was an important message about the local business culture he was supporting. The deeper messages are clear. Mi casa es su casa (my house is your house). We are committed together.

Skepticism shattered by turnabout

I recall one feedback meeting when the participant disagreed and expressed contempt at the thought that chocolate and color could affect being seen as inspirational. There were also several other issues surfaced by her respondents' feedback. On a long drive after meeting her, I experienced personal disappointment at not getting through to a person whom I thought was obviously facing difficulty. She was so convincing in her cynical view of the matter, that I actually questioned whether what I had heard from all the previous role models on inspiration around chocolate and color was somehow not representative of some meaningful awareness. The power of the cynic can get to me, if I let it.

These thoughts crossed my mind as I drove for five hours to the location for my next meeting. This leader was situated with the client in a large manufacturing plant. At one point during our meeting, I offered the idea of color and chocolate. I even mentioned the pattern of Hershey's miniatures, M&Ms and Reese's miniature peanut butter cups. If you ever wondered how the expression "his mouth dropped" originated, this leader would have clearly demonstrated. He actually turned speechless for a few seconds, as if he wanted to talk and could not.

When he recovered, he said, "Marty, the plant manager has a reputation for being inspirational. So much so, that I have approached him, as my client, and asked him if he would mentor me on being inspirational. If you were to go into his office, you would see lots of color, to include model train sets and other hobbies. And on his desk, he has three kinds of chocolate—Hershey's miniatures, M&Ms and Reese's miniature peanut butter cups."

There are several lessons that come from this actual story that could translate into other experiences we all share in life. That chocolate and color are what keys inspiration, or that there are three top kinds of chocolate, are not the lessons here, nor are they the reality. These are not the keys. The deeper messages are clear.

For those that like good news, this story continues. Months later, I revisited the site where I had met the master cynic. As a different leader and I began to share her feedback, she commented how much she was looking forward to this feedback meeting. She said their manager had participated in this previously and that dramatic changes had occurred since then. Their manager was more supportive, less negative and everyone had noticed a change throughout their teams as a result, according to this second participant leader.

The manager she referred to was indeed the leader I described as cynical, mentioned above. As I left, I stopped by that manager's office to say hello. She was out of the office. I could not help but notice a bowl of chocolates setting on her table. It was the very table we had used during our meeting to review her feedback.

Gender bias?

One area where a possible gender predisposition may exist is in the use of color and conversation pieces in the work place.

One male participant, a role model for inspiration, when including the colorful decor as one of the reasons he cited, concluded, "Marty, this isn't me!"

"What do you mean?"

"My wife and daughter came in one Saturday and said, 'Dad, we have to do something about your office.' I replied, 'Have at it,' and they did. The following weekend, they came in and decorated, and that Monday, it was like a line of people continually visiting to see my office. So I've kept it this way and have noticed a change in conversations ever since."

Following this revelation, for the few future participants who referred to the color in their office, I would ask them if they were responsible for that color themselves. Every woman said yes and every man said no, that it was some lady in their lives, whether their wife, daughter, female administrative assistant or friend.

Obviously, this would not hold true for all men and women, but it did lead me to hypothesize. Was it possible that the men were more geared to focusing on just the work and the women to including their environment? I did not see enough role model leaders to pursue this any further, but enough of a pattern began to develop and arouse my interest.

Miscellaneous additional quotes from the role models for motivation

Notice the richness of perspective, awareness, behavior and technique in each of the following comments from different role models for 'motivates.'

> "I change my voice tone automatically when I sense someone under tension, stress. I encouraged the practice of blowing soap bubbles at team meetings, because my people claim bubbles relieve tension, reduce stress and relax them to enable clearer thinking."

> "Sitting next to people is an example of working to live, not living to work."

> "It's the informal aspects that are more important than the formal aspects."

The informal aspects the participant leader is referring to here are spontaneous, unscheduled one-on-one conversations with employees. His experience is that these ongoing, informal chats have greater impact than the more formal, one-on-one conversation that is characterized by a strictly held to, predetermined agenda. However, the participant was still indicating that formal aspects have their place in the work setting.

> "It took work for me to remember to just say thanks to individuals, because there is always so much to do and I'm always so busy. It was a kind of personal tunnel vision—focused on what I'm doing— the reports due in, who's absent, what contracts are pending, etc. I gradually learned that a bonus is nice— it's like a shot in the arm. But a thank you becomes long lasting, ongoing. I'm genuinely sharing a reflection of you."

This previous point about genuinely sharing a reflection of another is one profound way of stating a core value behind verbally thanking another. It is presenting them a glimpse into a verbal mirror; reflecting a view of what that person is all about; reflecting their inner beauty and essence. For some of us reading this, if you prefer, substitute the word strength for the word beauty.

"My job is not just about cooking food for my employees and bringing in chocolates—it's about getting their day started off well." (This is an example of stating the deeper meaning, beyond the obvious.)

"Sitting next to people, I'm more relaxed, tend to let my guard down, which means I tend to let go of my prejudices and biases enough to hear most clearly."

"I teach workers how to lighten up, solve problems creatively; bring out the humor, look for the human side, find excuses to laugh. Acting happy makes you feel happier. Going through the motions can trigger the emotions inside…talking positively to people is a way to change. You begin acting the person you want to be."

"I never pass anyone's aisle, sensing their presence, without saying, 'Hi,' and acknowledging them."

"Am I still wearing the last bad experience I had on my face?"

"No matter what I'm doing, my door is open and I turn to greet you as my customer—all people. The empowering message is, our business passes through you, and when I delegate, people realize they had it to begin with."

"Sitting next to people, at an angle, not across from them, prevents distractions from distracting."

"One example is using a low set area on this floor which we call the pit. I'll leave a voice mail to the entire account (hundreds of people in this building), requesting they come meet me at the pit at 12:55 (p.m.). Those that can come, do. Then, I might stand up on a table and read an 'attaboy' just received from the client, then say to everybody, 'This is what we were talking about three months ago, remember? Here is an example of the results!' Everybody applauds, cheers and we go back to work. The word naturally gets out to the rest of the team."

✱ "People don't care how much you know, until they know how much you care."

Personal testament

One of my strengths in my own multi-rater feedback had been the behavior statement on motivation. At an empowerment workshop, done in the mid 1990s, years before I received that feedback, the workshop facilitator introduced an activity for us to complete. Since it was our work group that knew each other who attended, they had us write on a 5 by 8 index card for each person three to six qualities or characteristics we admired about that person that we considered strengths. On the index card (see figure 1) is the consolidated list of characteristics eight different people used to describe me. Each person's input is separated by a different color of ink. (Note: In the blue ink, "opt" signifies optimist.) Upon discovering this index card in my files, I immediately noticed the resemblance of input on that index card ("thanks people often") to the results of my motivation feedback within my multi-rater feedback years later. This correlated to the patterns of verbal appreciation that so clearly emerged from role model leaders for 'motivates' over the ensuing years.

Marty

IDEALIST

J.N.

THANKS OFTEN, CARES, FRIENDLY, MENTOR

good MENTOR

CONSIDERATE OF OTHERS

S.S.

Idealist/Opt.

Is people oriented

Thanks people often

Has good presentation skills

THANKS PEOPLE OFTEN

IS A GOOD LISTENER

IS SELF-CONFIDENT

CARES ABOUT PEOPLE

IS CONSIDERATE OF OTHERS

G.P.

HAS TRUE WISDOM

IS A LEADER

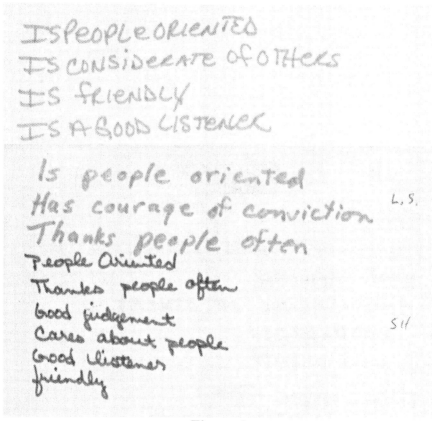

Figure 1

Just don't think about it

Sitting on a park bench one warm afternoon, I asked the question of my wife's great uncle Clarence, "How do you do it?" It felt awkward to ask. I had not planned on asking that question and I did not want to ask it like, "How have you managed to stay alive for so long?" It's not like I was rushing him or wanting him to think he was past due! So I simply asked him, "How do you do it?" This lively, active, yet gentle man of ninety years replied without hesitation, "Just don't think about it."

It was the kind of universally wise answer that you would expect from our seniors. He was too busy living life to think about his age, the aches and pains or to be paralyzed by fear. If I were to write his biography, his life would be characteristic of the bottle half full, not half empty.

As I listened to the role models answer the question of what they do or say to cause people to feel life, energy and motivation in their presence, I often noticed they had to consciously think about what it is they do so frequently. For many, they are verbally thanking people for little things all the time, without even thinking about it. Is that you? Do you often present a glimpse of that person's essence through a verbal mirror? Do people you know describe you as demonstrating this behavior?

Could there be some connection between Clarence and these business role models for motivation? Could the habits and actions of both even be prolonging their life expectancy in a physical way?

That is the subject of research.

What I have discovered and shared with you in these pages, I believe, is all about life. This is what persuades me to choose motivation as the lead chapter.

As you read on, note the overlaps to what role models say they do in some other areas of business leadership.

In association with you, what's your sense when people walk away—are they feeling life, or something other than life?

2

Strategic or Visionary Thinking

"There's no pancake with any two sides the same. How do you think you are perceived by the person on the other side of the situation?"

- Participant

Our instant gratification society today tends to include a focus on anything immediate. Immediate problem solving, quick crisis resolution, turnaround and need for an action orientation tends to both give us an illusion of great progress and contribute to a tactical, short-term focus.

By contrast, strategic or visionary capacity balances the here and now with an outward focus into the future. This converts a myriad of indicators and trends into one's planning and decision making, recognizing what is relevant, engaging uncertainty and ambiguity, and providing a direction that increases people's confidence and productivity.

In my five years of feedback coaching, I discovered that even among highly rated leaders in the people care, leadership and integrity categories of behaviors, often these same leaders were not regarded as high frequency practitioners of strategic or visionary thinking behaviors located elsewhere in their feedback survey. Being seen as a strategic or visionary thinker was one of those areas of practice that truly distinguishes the highest performing leaders from the high performing ones, or separates the men from the boys, the women from the girls.

To my surprise, some leaders in lower level, tactical, operational-focused roles of leadership were still able to demonstrate these behaviors. Some leaders in strategic, direction-setting roles of leadership were not frequently demonstrating these behaviors. Listening to these strategic/visionary role models reversed my previously held belief that environmental constraints greatly inhibited one's ability to demonstrate strategic thinking, visionary behaviors. And, as you will see, these role model practitioners make the connections of being strategic to promoting collaboration, empowerment, trust and change.

Behaviors include fostering productive debate and conversation; promoting innovative thinking and problem solving; constructively challenging status quo thinking and assumptions; communicating the depth and breadth of the business; identifying opportunities for continual business growth; creating a shared vision; and using innovative ideas and perspectives to achieve results.

So what did I hear the role model leaders in varying environments, of varying age and educational background, indicate they do or say to cause all their respondents to mark them so highly?

The most often mentioned responses sounded like this conversational sequence:

> "Marty, I'm always asking questions of others."
> "What kinds of questions?"
> "Questions like: What other possibilities are there? How else could we look at this? Is there a way to ask the (or this) question differently?"

On the last comment, I asked one of the participants if they would give me a generic example of asking the question differently. His background was in psychology. He replied, "Sure, multiple-choice questions. When we grew up in the schools, especially in

Western society, we were conditioned to respond to the question, 'What's the right answer, (a), (b), (c) or (d)?' The quicker and more right we were in giving the right answer, the better off. We were rewarded with stars, A's for grades, verbal teacher praise and otherwise recognized as smart, studious and reliable. So, another way to ask a multiple-choice question, the same question differently, is to ask, 'In what situations is choice (a) the better answer? In what scenarios might (b) be the better response? When might (c) or (d) be the better solution? It's getting people to think out of their box and both challenging and developing their thinking beyond just memorizing."

Yet again, more on motivation

Another example of this returns us to motivation. One leader's point was that in asking the question differently, all questions were important, and the alternative ones even better qualified the original questioning. His example was that a typical way one might ask a question on motivation is, "How can I motivate others?" When asking it this way, it causes us to think about all the things we can do to influence motivating another person and we tend to look outwardly from ourselves. We look at things outwardly external to ourselves, such as salary, pay/benefits, perks, where we sit (office or window view versus sitting near the inner aisle with its high volume of indoor pedestrian traffic) and time off.

We can also ask an alternative question: "What is it I do, or what thoughts do I think about prior to doing, that prevents people from feeling motivated?" When asking the question in this manner, we tend to also look inwardly and think about the things that we can control more directly. Both questions are important. Answers to these questions will also surface over time, not necessarily all at once. The point I hear being made is that asking the alternative question also completes, or makes better, the original question. Our responses present us with a more complete perspective on the subject, in this case, motivation.

As you will notice later in this chapter, the various comments reflect a very distinctive opinion among the visionary role models against the general usage of a question starting with the word "why."

Other visionary practices

Beyond the emphasis on asking questions, role model leaders additionally credited these following habits for being perceived so frequently as demonstrating strategic/visionary behaviors.

Simplifying

Some participants indicated that simplifying the complexity of things by paraphrasing or sharing stories and analogies, also helped people to see the big picture. This enabled people to have more productive conversations around complex topics or issues that became simpler to see, understand and talk about.

Examples or comments about analogies leaders gave include:

"If you continue to steer a car looking right over the hood, it becomes taxing and you can't steer. You must be looking at different things in different ways. So, too, at work."

"Small adjustments of rudder changes affect the course over the long term."

"Yes, you are apprehensive about being portrayed before your time as an expert to the customer; yet among little trees, you are a redwood."

"Stories and analogies draw a crowd, which means people are thinking, similar to what the biblical Jesus did, sharing stories and analogies to get people to think."

"We need you to be the lineman for this presentation. Let him be the quarterback, the presenter to the customer. When the questions get too tough, we need you as our lineman to step up and handle the interference." (On using a football analogy to help people see how they can best contribute as part of a team.)

"Encouraging and sharing stories and analogies is networking and leveraging the varied experiences of the team, which is the true value of a team. This is what they mean when they say intellectual curiosity, or thought leadership in practice. We get beyond the canned terms and phrases to what it means."

"Creating analogies engages people, sells the vision."

"Taking what is complex and portraying as simple is getting to the heart of the issue and opens up people's minds."

Offering alternatives in conversation

"Here are the options as I see it, (a), (b) and (c). I recommend (b), but these are the options."

"I always think, if I do this, what will happen? This, that and maybe these things."

"I usually ask, 'What do you think if this or that were to happen?' I avoid the trap of giving them the answer or of not allowing enough time to promote productive debate and discussion."

"Asking the question differently empowers and motivates by getting people involved, thinking through multiple choices."

"If you get 'No' for an answer, paraphrase the question differently. Exploring alternatives paves the way for collaboration…funnels to the common ground. Then, explore, and build from there."

"When people approach me about things I have an answer to, I come across like—'Have you thought about trying this? Have you considered doing that?' I'm leaving them alternatives and options. I tend to simplify, to be spontaneous with brainstorming, reverse role-play, think in terms of alternatives, anything to promote people thinking more broadly, out of the box."

Reverse role-play refers to a practice of getting people to take on the role of another party, particularly their adversarial party, or to play the role from the opposite viewpoint. The role player converses on an issue, representing the interests of the other position. This promotes a broader understanding, encourages empathy, increases the potential to think of innovative solutions and more confidently prepares the role player. One example a participant leader offered involved his employees. He would tell them, "You play our customer and I'll play myself, the account manager, coming to you as our customer with this proposal for additional services." Here, the account manager gets to rehearse and practice with his employees, who know their customer. The employees get to increase their awareness and knowledge of their customer by putting themselves in their customer's shoes and talking the customer's talk. This produces what I call a ripple effect. Ripple effects include an increased ability of this team to anticipate customers' needs, to confidently interact with them and to achieve results. Other ripple effects benefiting the leader include developing his people and identifying back-ups, so the leader can eventually take a vacation with a peace of mind or move on in his own career. More thorough preparation increases the leader's self-confidence in advance of meeting the customer. <u>Additionally, the employees gain a better appreciation for how their leader is contributing to the team in ways that are typically transparent or unknown to employees.</u> The ripples continue, just as the ripples of tiny waves continue in the water at the point where we had tossed in a stone. Tiny ripples at the workplace combine to become visible and significant over time. The beneficial effects continue on after the role-play has been completed. Yes, the bottle can be half full.

"Asking questions from several different angles—from the customer, the employees, the department, the business, the financial and from a risk/benefits angle."

"Playing out the different models—if this, then what? It's like working a puzzle, like algebra. You could solve it for X, or solve it for Y or for Z. What variables could change to influence the outcomes? What are my actions? What are my outcomes?"

"It's making life an essay test, versus a true-false or multiple-choice job test. The means of strategy is in looking for solutions versus precise answers."

"Asking the same question differently—you are giving up your position, your personal investment with its emotional attachment, because it's a different question. Instead of repeating myself, showing upset when not understood, I would ask the question differently."

Inviting external person or people

Several leaders commented on inviting some external person or people into their team meeting, even if it's just telephonically.

"We were trying to grow business in Europe and I found a contact there willing to call in when we were brainstorming on this as a team. With his participation and his asking us, 'Have you thought about trying this or considered doing that,' and voicing thought starters, it helped our team to share ideas, increased our confidence and lead to a much better plan which proved fruitful."

While only providing the one participant's comment here, there were several leaders who commented on this aspect of inviting someone external into their team meetings when appropriate. This promoted a diversity of perspective, prompted team members thinking out of their box and cultivated more fertile ground for the seeds of external cooperation to take root.

Visionary leaders highlighted the virtues of brainstorming

However, they did so with a purpose and awareness of timing and patience. Their thoughts and examples of questions when brainstorming follow.

"I'll give so much time to diverging, encouraging people to think out of their box, to think of possibilities. I keep a sense of timing and follow my instincts as to when it is time to converge and bring it back. I'll then say something like, 'What do we now know that we did not know a few minutes ago?'"

"Brainstorming often occurs on the fly and is spontaneous, not necessarily limited to the scheduled agenda of a meeting. Some brainstorming occurs in the hallway. It stimulates thinking and people feel involved." (This is another example of an advantage the informal aspects of leading can present over the formal aspects.)

"You push them into the third party—step out of the situation and evaluate it, versus still being inside the situation, reacting to it. You get people to evaluate it as a test through asking 'what-focused' questioning."

✳ "We often think in a rut. Instead of thinking just what we already know, you start with the end result."

"I'm always engaging others in conversation—presenting options to my directs, and we talk through these options."

✳ "To have another good idea, you must leave your last one and not be possessive of your last good idea."

✳ "Live in the question, not the answer. Always ask, 'What else is there?'"

"'Can you think of a way that would be better?' Or I'll ask, 'What changes would you make to this?'"

"If we can do this, we could do that. What do you think? There's always a pony in here somewhere. I try to create alternatives and protect people's integrity, esteem and the business."

✳ "Answers to 'what' and 'how' questions tend to expound. Answers to 'why' questions tend to be one line, short answers."

"If typically preoccupied, say when I'm fixing something that is wrong, I am more focused, more after the fact. When not preoccupied, I am more open, observant, relaxed and I'm enquiring more. I don't find myself cutting people off. It starts with a chosen state of mind."

"If you were the leader, if it was your company, what would you do?"

"Brainstorming creates the buy-in, before the change forces us. I share all I can."

"How would you like to see it handled?"

✱ "Brainstorming anticipates change." *god forbid.*

✱ "Spontaneity of asking questions is an expression of curiosity. Curiosity and spontaneity are sisters."

"I would never ask 'why' if I truly wanted to hear what they're trying to say. 'Why' or 'but' and 'so' are pillar expressions of the close-minded."

"I go through an opportunity pipeline. Think about what ifs, then determine best courses of action and tie objectives to our business plan."

"Asking open-ended questions about future events is proactive planning."

"I prefer to hear a dissenting opinion other than my own opinion—this nurtures my personal growth."

"I always establish a context for people. If it is a reusable thing, then it's strategic. If it's a throwaway solution, then it's tactical."

"To the continued 'Yes, but,' I'll say 'OK, if that were absent, what would you do?'"

Drawing

By drawing, the role models do not mean being an artist is a prerequisite for being a visionary. They emphasize that a visual, even a rough one scrawled on a whiteboard or piece of paper, or encouraging others to draw, promotes a more strategic, bigger picture view.

"This is what I want—what do you need from me? I'll draw a picture of a plant (industrial) layout, raw materials into and product out from, and say, 'Here are the holes, the weak areas.' I'll tell them, 'Don't focus on what you have, focus on what you don't have...the devil is in the details. Don't get involved in the details. <u>Sell the concept</u>.'"

It was not until some time later that I realized the following comment from a role model summarizes this topic on other visionary practices.

"These are word associations describing strategic/visionary traits: to simplify through the use of stories and analogies; to brainstorm and involve others. Drawing, developing straw man solutions, using spontaneity, asking alternative questions, anticipating and proposing alternatives."

Environmental influence

When providing feedback early on as a coach, I would hear from leaders exceptionally low in strategic or visionary thinking that it was due to their environment. They were leading in a role requiring daily delivery to specific contract requirements. They worked in a manufacturing plant, or worked in a financial environment beset by regulations and procedures, or they were there to ensure that tactical, operational requirements were met or exceeded. These leaders indicated they did not have time for being strategic or visionary and that that was for their leaders to accomplish.

Then I shared feedback with a leader who was also very tactical, with a short-term view and operational focus, by his admission. He even indicated that our meeting might be interrupted by some emergency and was that "doable?" I could almost always tell when a request was legitimate. In this case, he was acknowledging a part of his normal environment, and I had the added advantage of already knowing the strength of his feedback report.

When we came to the visionary section, where his respondents also marked him a role model, I mentioned to him how his peers before him in similar positions stated this did not apply to their role and they had no time to display these strategic/visionary behaviors. He laughed in response and said, "Marty, I have discovered that most people think visionary is something separate from what they do at their level. They see it as something **apart** from their role, rather than being **a part of** their work. Being visionary or strategic has everything to do with their role. When my people come in here with an emergency, I'll stand right up, come over here to the whiteboard with them (we were in his office), and somebody already knows to grab a marker, and they are drawing out the problem on the board. And I'm asking them questions like, 'What other possibility could be behind this? Is there another way for us to look at this? What do you think? Does this establish a precedent?' I'll listen, try to articulate back through what I'm hearing, or say, 'Have you thought about this?'"

I learned from this person that the strategic really complements, or enhances, the tactical, operational activities and solutions. There is a life-giving relationship here. I learned that varying environments could present more constraints than others for strategic/innovative thinking, yet we, as leaders, have more ability to impact and take advantage of visionary thinking than we give ourselves credit for. It really comes down more often to our habits and how we are used to doing and behaving.

More teachings from the visionaries among us

The word spontaneity surfaced as a trait that strategic/visionary role model leaders often shared. These leaders had the ability to adapt to changing situations without insisting on sticking with the original plan, as they sensed something larger and more important occurring. Sometimes, they would change the location of a meeting mid-stream, to help complete a change in the content of the conversation from, for example, talking about organizational silos and switching to talking about people care subjects. I listened to a speech given by Valerie Oberlie, a senior vice president of Walt Disney sometime in the late 1990s. She was addressing a convention of people focused on creative problem solving. She made the points that they, in Disney, never inspired breakthroughs through the use of rule books, which invite rigidity. They had no rulebooks because they had accomplishments to achieve. She further asked the question, "How does spontaneity become established in an organization?" In response, she indicated that Disney gave their employees only one objective—to use their good judgment. There were no other rules. Incorporating the business angle, she commented that this becomes empowering and encourages their employees, whom they refer to as their cast, to provide for their guests' needs with the best treatment and the most creative solutions. *How many handbooks, standard details, rule books does THA have? Is strict rigidity the best quality control? Or even the best inspiration for new ideas? No.*

Asking "what" and "how" questions, over "why" questions

The visionary role model leaders emphasized the asking of questions starting with the word "what" or "how," as opposed to asking a question starting with the word "why." In their book *Smart Work*, Lisa Marshall and Lucy Freedman suggest that asking "what" and "how" questions will enable you to hear what happened and draw your own conclusions. A "why" question will elicit people's interpretations. So asking "what" and "how" questions enables you to form your own conclusions and not be limited to accepting another's interpretation. They further suggest that a "why" question tends to draw a more emotional response from others. By example, if in response to hearing a person say, "This situation is hopeless," you ask, "Why is that?", there is more of a tendency to hear a more emotionally charged response, such as, "They're jerks, that's why." Instead, to the statement "This situation is hopeless," you reply, "What makes you say that?" The response tends to be more objective, less emotional.

Robert Fritz, in his book *The Path of Least Resistance*, speaks to the power of asking, "What do I want" or "What result do I want to create?" in developing a creative orientation in our lives. He notes that the "how" question gets us process, not result. As an initial question, he maintains you are limited to results that are directly related to what you already know how to do. He summarizes by saying that if you ask the "how" before the "what" question, you can only create variations of what you already have. I conclude from this that how questions are good, when the timing is right. In other words, if we are always asking the "how" question before the "what," we are limiting the results to what we already know.

I was hearing the visionary role model leaders repeatedly emphasize asking "what" and "how" questions and, as I read Fritz' book, was astounded by the similarity of what I was reading to what I was hearing from the role models. Little did I know I was to become even more astonished. While keeping a copy of the book in my possession, I met a leader marked "role model" for visionary. To my question, "What do you think you do or say?" he replied, "I am always asking a 'what' question before a 'how' question, and never a 'why' question."

Believing in coincidence, I pulled out my copy of Fritz' book and exclaimed, "You've read this book." He replied that he had never seen that book before. "Then how did you learn about this?" His response, "Marty, I just learned over time that when people get in disagreements and then I use a 'what' question, it draws people to the common denominator of what they are all about, trying to accomplish and can agree on. Once they understand the 'what,' they can more readily figure out the 'how' and tolerate others doing it differently. It's recognizing that it's in the 'how' where the diversity is so rich."

This became one of the unique benefits of my experience as a feedback coach. I heard role models cite the very practices that I could map to the ideas offered in some books, such as those authored by Lisa Marshall, Lucy Freedman and Robert Fritz.

What about you?

When you talk with others, what is your sense? What do you hear yourself more often asking—a question that starts with the word "what," or "how" or "why?" This question was among those that helped participants initially puzzled over lower perceptions across strategic/visionary or communication behaviors to clarify how they were contributing to those lower perceptions. I often heard them indicate "why" as their habit of beginning their questioning. This again shows the good news, that improvement or slight change in one area of behavior or habit can reap benefits across groupings of different behaviors, such as behaviors in strategic thinking, communication and, as we will soon see, resolving conflict.

When sharing feedback with a participant who was born and raised on the other side of the Iron Curtain, I shared with him similar insights on the impact of "why" questions. His response was, "It is the same for us over here in our language."

I once met with a Canadian leader who shared with me the feedback he had received years previously from a different feedback tool. On noticing his high marks for strategic/visionary behaviors, I asked him what leads to that being so high, even if we were to assume it remained so to that current day. His reply—"I ask a lot of 'what' questions." I could only smile to myself, in order to contain my continuing astonishment.

Here's what some leaders who were rated **lower** in the visionary category had to say.

> "Someone talks to me, I only say, 'OK,' and do not think to ask the follow-up questions."

> "I tend to not simplify for others, because I am so focused on the details."

"I always ask 'why?' of others, and now I am beginning to really understand how I am continually limiting the conversations. My wife and (teenage) kids had been telling me this for years. Now work is telling me the same message, but I never realized it until now."

"My meetings are planned, structured, with little or no spontaneous conversation."

"I'm in the 'These are the symptoms, how do we go fix them?' comfort zone."

Resolving conflict

Even though resolving conflict comes later in this book, the role model leaders for "visionary" often drew a connection with these practices to helping to resolve conflict. This is an example of how the various behaviors and practices for these behaviors begin to overlap. This also presents us with a positive multiplication of benefit, since improvement in any one area will have a reciprocal benefit in other areas. We have already noted some comments from visionary leaders around handling the "yes, but" or "why," and other uses of our language that tend to derail conversations into a win-lose, or lose-lose proposition.

A few role model leaders have separately introduced me to the concept of starting with a straw man document to resolve conflict or divert internal power struggles. One example was a leader recalling being asked to facilitate a group of people who represented diverse interests and were in conflict. In this scenario, rather than introduce the contentious group to a blank sheet of paper, flip chart or computer screen for generating ideas from a clean slate, the leader chose to introduce starter ideas on what he called a straw man document. Reminding people what it was they were trying to accomplish together, this leader directed their attention to the document and invited feedback and critique. Instead of the group members critiquing each other's new ideas, they became unified in critiquing and developing a solution out of the initial straw man proposal. They were critiquing ideas up there in front of the room, not critiquing each other.

Consider the following additional comments from visionary leaders on reducing conflict.

"Saying 'what' in place of 'why' marginalizes the harshness."

"I'll play role reversal, encourage others to play devil's advocate or to play the other party. This also helps in resolving conflict, much less seeing the bigger picture."

"I'll give people a context, communicate a purpose, how they are contributing, they are appreciated for...not just complete these five tasks."

"Find ways to say 'yes' creatively. Getting us from why can't we to why can we. It's always about understanding what interests them. Take what they are asking you, link it to what they are interested in, then rephrase the question differently to get to the win-win."

"Big picture defuses the situation."

"There is no pancake with any two sides the same. How do you think you are perceived by the person on the other side of the situation?"

"Accountability is looking downstream for the effect of decisions we make today."

"If the meeting moderator cuts the chit-chat to start precisely at the scheduled one o'clock start time with the business agenda, the meeting tends to become more tense, less open, less ideas, less innovation."

"I learned to switch from saying things like, 'That's a good idea, but…,' to saying things like, 'How else could we do that? Any other thoughts?' etc."

To conclude this chapter on strategic/visionary thinking, what follows are samples of a variety of short responses. If being a visionary and exhibiting strategic thinking is an area of interest and potential further development for you, read on. We can look beyond the limitations of our own spoken language to see how different habits and ways of communicating can make us more effective and further the benefits of strategic thinking.

"I ask a lot (of questions) up front, but the payoff comes months later. If you do this today, how will this make life easier a year down the road? If we do this, will it lay the groundwork for _____?"

"I didn't used to be seen, or ever see myself, as a visionary in former years because I always needed a payoff of personal pride by proclaiming, 'See? I got it. I know it,' from way back in school days. Once I changed that behavior, my payoff became to get others to a point where they're saying, 'I got it. I've arrived!'"

How many of us recall taking pride in being among the first to get it, to correctly answer in school? If so, could that habit be surfacing in how we communicate today? For example, could that habit be at the source of our cutting others off in conversation? Is there any downside to being quick with the answer that limits our relationship with others; that limits our ability to draw out the potential and development of others around us? Is there an adjustment we can make to still respect our strength and also diminish the downside?

"I always look at how things could be, not how they are."

"I used to be fact based, but have lately balanced that with more creative, idea based thinking."

"I use a bridge to the present when talking about the future and possibilities, plus, I keep things prioritized and keep that visible to people over time."

"Visionary requires some aspects of a democratic style of leadership."

"I get people out of their box, out of them/us, through job shadowing and promoting camaraderie."

"People don't get up each morning to do dumb things, they act on the information life provides them. So educate them on the big picture and ask, 'Does this make sense?' Explain your thought process in a nonadversarial way."

"Questions like, 'What do you think we can do to resolve this? What can we do to benefit the end user?'"

"To get in tune with the bigger picture and with trends, I sit in on others' teleconferences, such as those of customers and of teleconferences representing multiple groups."

"It's being and thinking 'can do' over 'can't do.'"

"You need to do this with lips and ears, not with the crutch of presentation materials. It's more relationship."

"It's about communicating perspective—losing your job, yes, that's bad. Losing your family, that's worse."

"What are the data points, not just the one data point? I always begin with the strategy 'what do we want,' and then the 'how,' say, 'Do we employ the nickel defense?'" (Using a football analogy as an example here.)

"To willingly challenge is a by-product of my enthusiasm, energy and of addressing concerns."

"I'll ask 'What's the short-term impact? What are the long-term implications? What's the impact on the customer?'"

"I look for all the ways to make it work. This is not just about seeing it half full or half empty, not just about asking, 'Why not?'. This is bigger than that."

"Most are so buried in their work, they don't read all the messages of changes in the company or how the industry is changing. I make it my business to understand."

"Effectively challenging the status quo is thinking it through from both sides, the pros and the cons."

"Cannot micromanage to do this. This is about asking questions; analysis of what are the business drivers, versus micromanaging. Set the tone versus the details. This is empowering, as well."

"What are the different alternatives you've considered and what have we done to verify, explore and test...what question are we trying to ask? What are we trying to solve?"

In Their Presence: Best Practices and Stories of Role Models

"You write the question out that you see in your own words, your own terms, just colloquial, and we begin to see the similarities."

"Yes, this is the way it is today, and we can't change today. But how about tomorrow...through our career planning, what we choose to talk about. Plus, I'll use analogies." (On introducing the proactive in a reactive mindset.)

"When people commonly pick on words, parts of ideas, then they're only seeing little pieces and not seeing the whole."

"Diverge the conversation when the options appear limited, then converge naturally when you sense you have more to choose from."

✷ "I start with, 'What do you want to do?'"

✷ "When personalities get in the way, go to common sense and common goal."

✷ "I stay informed, read industry magazines, articles, the Internet, and pass on what is relevant, potentially useful. It means nothing unless I do that."

"Our perspective is limited to what we see. There's the story of the guide taking blindfolded people into the jungle who says, 'Put your hands on this and tell me what it is.' One felt the trunk of an elephant and said, 'A fire hose.' One felt the tail and said, 'A garden hose.' They were all correct, based on their limited perspective of what they can see."

"It's tying in decisions today with future customer satisfaction."

"How the question is asked will influence the answer or information we get."

"I'm adaptable, will respond to others calmly and keep order, instead of causing others to respond to me. I'm the sanity check, the litmus test, and I provide the rationale. I try to accommodate. When you scream, I can't hear you. Meaning, the intent of what they're trying to say gets lost in the emotion."

"I used to always throw out the idea first; now, I first ask them, 'What do you think?'"

"I'm constantly challenging the status quo. 'Did we try this, what about...?' Plus, I'll use humor, way-out thinking, carefree thinking, risk taking. 'Now what are we going to do different today, to put action into this?'"

"What I do in my job is to generate ideas that motivate people to action."

"Need a framework of trust, not a checklist."

"As a matter of time management, I give one hour per week to looking through my professional magazines. However, I key on the advertisement pages, not the articles. Something catches my eye and I think back to a comment or need expressed by the customer in a meeting. I'll ask my technical people, 'Does this say what I think it's saying?' They'll make the call to the 1-800 number to investigate. As a result, on a few occasions, over time, we have proposed more alternatives and choices to the customer that have saved them lots of money. For example, I'll say, 'We can do (a) or (b), or if you can do without this one feature you requested, I can provide this, which is already developed and out there, at some significant cost savings, instead of developing it in-house.' The customer thinks it over and will say to go for the latter."

"I'm all about how do we do things differently, and they (their employees or extended team members) will be nominated to implement. I'm negotiating an idea with a person, will say something like, 'That's an even better idea.' They're enthusiastic. It culminates in our reply to the customer. 'Here's a response to your proposal, and the price, and here's a recommendation to change what you asked for.'"

"Insanity is doing the same thing again and expecting different results."

"Either procrastination or focusing on little things first are the opposites of acting on vision and risk taking. The little things will always keep coming, keeping you otherwise preoccupied."

"I can quickly see the big picture, the order of sequence of events, what's important."

Next, does strategic or visionary thinking relate to taking risks and decisiveness in the workplace? Can having a broad picture, long-term view increase the effectiveness of daily decisions?

3

Risk Taking/Decisiveness

"Decisiveness and risk taking are sisters to the visionary/strategic. Deciding and taking risks is the follow-through that completes the work of the visionary."

- Participant

Role model leaders for risk taking behaviors often sounded similar to the visionary role model leaders in what they practiced. Indeed, they indicated that behaviors like the following received their energy from the strategic and visionary categories of behaviors.

Behaviors include facing difficult situations with steadfastness and courage; making sound decisions in adversity; showing confidence to defend an unpopular decision; taking risks by trying out new ideas and approaches; welcoming discovery by sustaining new ideas; encouraging others to try new ideas; acting with appropriate urgency; making sound judgments even without all the information; and making the right decision based on the situation.

One pattern of role model responses centered around the means to communicating decision making among their various respondents. It goes like this:

"I'm always asking a question of others like, 'What's the worst that could happen?' And they know I don't mean death. It's usually a quick brainstorm. 'If we were to try this, what could go wrong?'

"Let's say they indicate '(a).' I'll continue, 'What else?' They could say '(b).' 'Good, what else?...Well that's still really (b), agree? What else?...OK, (c). Is there anything else we can think of?'

"Then, we review and evaluate the constraints that were identified. 'If (a) were to happen, would that prevent us from doing X? No? Then if (b) were to occur, would that prevent us from doing this? Yes, (b) is a showstopper. If (c) were to become a reality, would that prevent us from doing X?'

"Let's say we determine (c) occurring will not prevent us. Then I'll say something like, 'Let's go back to (b). Are there any workarounds, any temporary process or fix we could devise, any communication we could develop?'

"Often, I'll hear others thoughtfully comment, 'So what you say we are really trying to do with X is to...' People walk away from this usually brief conversation with a more complete understanding of the 'what,' and feel (and act) more confident, anticipating worst-case scenarios in advance. They become less inclined to keep checking back with me for little things. Any one of us may ask, 'What did we just learn from this?' We develop a plan, and we move on. The problems that do occur may not always be the exact ones we predicted, but they are usually some derivative of what we thought about."

The summary point of this leader, and others like him, was that asking the question and engaging relevant people in this kind of conversation led to ownership, empowerment and a clearer understanding of the big picture among the key players. Follow-on issues and problems were resolved against a backdrop of perspective. To me, this is an example of competitive difference occurring in little ways over time, with "relatively brief" conversations. It's an example of working a broader, big picture perspective into conversations each day. For teams otherwise equal in technological know-how and tools, the team with this perspective and practice has the advantage. And again, this activity has multiplying impacts on people's morale, productivity, confidence, commitment, desire, and you, the reader, can complete this sentence from your own experience!

Another risk taker indicated something similar, saying, "Always start with the end result. Then, what are the possibilities if 'yes'? What are the possibilities if 'no'? Thinking outcomes, thinking in the future, there is usually a differentiator that jumps out."

Much of the aim of risk takers in business naturally focuses around benefiting the client, as the following comments from different risk taker role model leaders indicate.

> "When the client asks, 'Can you do this?' I say, 'Yes, and here's the risk.' I rarely say no."

> "The client can't say yes if we haven't already asked, 'What's the worst that can happen?'"

> "I'm always asking, 'What problem are we trying to solve? Is there a problem? What business need fills this request? What makes the client request this?'"

> "I combine relevant information with relevant experience for better decisions. If I do this, what does it mean for the client? For me? For my staff? For the company?"

Coaching

Coaching provided by leaders can be one method the highly decisive leaders use to develop their employees in decisiveness and risk taking.

"I tell them, 'I can help you with that decision, but I think you already have the answer. If we just change roles, you be me, and I'll play the customer.' I'll even change chairs with them." (This is an example of role reversal.)

"A response of mine might be: 'What makes you ask me these questions? Are you really seeking approval, or are you afraid to take a risk, or is it some combination of the two?'"

"To accelerate people's confidence in deciding and in their risk taking ability, I'll say, 'Leave your identification badge at the door, you are all me today. What would you change if you were me?' I'll have them sit in my office chair and rotate our roles. I start them with a context, a background, not a textbook. I'll use scenarios from our business application and then role-play in team meetings. This is like being on the sidelines, where mistakes are OK. It's not the pressure of being on the playing field and having to perform accordingly."

"Checkpoints built into the plan allowing for a change in course are essential, rather than go all the way to the end. Checkpoints lessen their frustration, and what takes place as a result of checkpoints becomes accepted behavior, instead of a perception they'll be seen as wrong or erratic."

"What would you do, choose or decide if it were your call?"

🌟 "I'm decisive, but I do not make decisions for other people. They grow by their decisions. I'll mentor them. For example, help them build an argument for justifying."

"I coach my people to always review, look back, really understand what was good and bad, then look forward based on that knowledge and adjust."

❋ "I have them establish what are the critical success factors, or critical decision factors, weighed against the criteria. Then they produce options and then we can decide."

"I teach them there's a time for thinking and a time for acting, and their ability to recognize the difference is key."

What follows are further tidbits of wisdom, tips and practices captured from the role model leaders for "risk taking" and "decisiveness." These reflect the inner thinking and external workings of those perceived as high decisive and as high risk takers. If this last phrase, as high risk takers, leaves you with a bad taste in your cranial juices, that may be the first thing to explore for yourself. I believe self-awareness is one of the factors that distinguishes an average performer from a role model. Take these next two comments from role models as an example of the fruits of self-awareness.

🌟"When I am overly tired and worn, I tend to want more and more data and certainty before making a decision and I go less with my intuition. This just adds more and more to my work pace, to my fatigue, and to the fatigue of others around me. It becomes a reinforcing loop."

"I changed **from** sounding like, 'Here's the background. Let's talk about this,' **toward** saying,

'Here's the background. Unless I hear from you, here's what I'll do.'"

"First, do not look for the answers. Look first for the questions, then the answer usually comes."

"We are sometimes intimidated by questions, afraid they'll embarrass us, or that we'll ask stupid questions. We need humor. We take ourselves way too seriously. Asking questions and making effective decisions are also affected by how much we have to do."

"Let's think now, administratively, which one administratively makes sense? Operationally? Logistically? Tactically? Strategically?"

"'What did I learn from this?' means 'What's our plan to move on?' We're going to have problems; the standard of excellence is not the absence of problems, but it's how we respond technically, emotionally."

✳ "If you are too worried about making the right decision, then you can't take risks."

"The lower my confidence (in making decisions and taking risks), the lower the commitment level and stake of others. The higher my confidence, the greater their commitment level. This gets repeated in small ways every day."

✳"Mistake-free equals risk-free equals indecisive. I seek leaders making a mistake, which means they are moving forward, not sitting and waiting for something to happen."

"When risk adverse, I seek control, safety and comfort over discomfort and a feeling of failure. When I follow my gut instincts, making decisions, then I have received feedback that I have a more inspirational effect as well."

✳ "Maintaining status quo leads to short-term decisions."

"I rarely make a decision for someone else. For example, in career planning and the person moving on. How you position yourself for mobility is not just my problem as a leader. I'll ask them a question like, 'Do you have all your processes documented? No? Well, we have until May.'"

"Worst decision is no decision—you can try to build consensus, then GO. You can always adjust."

"What's the probability? What's the benefit? What's the risk? Translated, there are your alternatives being developed."

"Asking them to solve their own problems is showing trust. Asking, 'What can we do with that?' keeps them at ease and stimulates."

"I'm always asking, 'What have we learned?' in a roundtable, which encourages stories and analogies being shared."

"First ask, 'Where are we now?' Next ask, 'Where do we want to be?' Then, going backwards becomes logical, because I know what the roadmap is. I can take risks that aren't as risky now."

"'I don't have enough data' is no longer an excuse. There is always plenty of data."

✳ "Decisiveness first starts with asking the questions and listening."

"The arbitrariness of making decisions is essential to causing an action to happen. Make an arbitrary one and manage to it. It's either right or adjust if it's wrong."

"The group does not decide, but the group provides the perspective."

"The risk taker considers but does not dwell on the consequences. Risk adverse people worry, frown and are stressful. What is different from when you were young that reduced your propensity to risk?"

"Look at pros and cons, yes; but look for more. Look for the win-win. Look for the positives in the cons, too. Focus on what solution is best based on the facts as you know them."

"Typically, continue questioning after the first answer or response, yet do so courteously. Getting additional data, for example, a cost model with negative indicators, turns a 'That's just the way it is' into a 'You're asking me to sign a piece of business not good for the company.'"

"Anticipate every bad thing that could happen and document some contingencies."

"Which problem would we rather live with?"

"We can find one hundred reasons why this won't work; we just need to find one reason that it will. What have you already tried?"

"I never have as much information as I'd like to have, so I just go with my gut."

"I analyze top to bottom, not bottom to top. What's the general direction, rough analysis of where to go, and let people run with it."

"Integrity includes integrity to making decisions."

"Used to be, since I had an 'all or nothing' tendency, if something was so huge I couldn't do it all in one day, then I'd choose nothing, procrastinate, not decide. I learned I'll never have more time tomorrow than today." (On time management)

"If you can't draw your issues or solution, you don't understand it well."

"I don't blame. They have my full support. I understand others' views. I look at the antagonists and examine their motives, not think about how they're a jerk. How to figure them out, like figuring out the fox. I'm honest and blunt with the client."

"It's both digging in and letting go of issues/timelines/decisions needed—when people know and show awareness, then I back off."

"No decision is a poor decision. Can always adjust later."

"Nothing in my e-mail remains without response for more than 24 hours."

"If there is too much to do, then choose what is critical."

"Considering the implications of decisions is the intersection of integrity with decisiveness, while showing confidence."

"Always ask, 'What are we going to do about it?'"

"The risk of personal failure scares most people. It is almost totally absent in my mind. For me, it's a leap of faith revisited over and over. I do not agonize over a decision and prefer not to think about it as I let it simmer. Then I purposefully wake up, say I will or I won't. The goal makes it preordained. Even if I do not understand the event at the time, I know I will come out on the other side, and looking back, can better adjust."

"Ambiguity is a continuum. You will always NOT have all the information. Remain open to changing course later. Take action; deal with problems as you go along."

"Tradeoff is there will be some frustration due to some rework. Even then, you are still learning. The returns outweigh any losses."

"A clue to being decisive is in a person's initial response to a request. People dread hearing, 'I'll give you an answer later,' compared to, 'Here's what we'll do,' the immediate answer. This exemplifies and puts into action the wise saying, 'Better to ask for forgiveness than for permission.'"

"I base decisions on dissension. Tell me what you are thinking and do not sugarcoat it. We're in the huddle here, and people can relate to that analogy. In the huddle, we decide to do this, then, as the quarterback, one causes all to go execute."

"Determining first things first is about prioritizing, and it's about the tradeoffs. Secondary things you do not do, they are what somebody else can do. Knowing what's important, prioritizing what is the MOST important. Know the details of the MOST and act on it."

"What's the worst that could happen—do nothing, or accept responsibility and document?"

"A person cannot take on all that they possibly can, unless they take on more than they can possibly achieve."

"I take care of people things first. Whether cellphone or e-mail, they would not be calling unless they needed me. I'll ask, 'What's the problem?' Talk it through with them, and encourage them to make a decision. Then back them up to my boss."

"Recognize the point of diminishing returns. Then cut your losses, learn and move on."

"It's actually replacing the hierarchy of position with the hierarchy of ideas."

"Life is all about deciding, and you never have all the data. When you don't decide, you're not living."

"We are either moving forward or backward, but we are not standing still."

Challenging the perfectionist within us

I listened to Margaret Wheatley, an accomplished author and consultant, talk about a scientific theory called chaos theory, and I believe it applies here in decisiveness and risk taking.

Briefly, I heard Margaret describe chaos theory as originating from observations that some scientists make. When they observe nature and the universe through the eyes of science, they observe chaos. Yet, they observe patterns of order emerge out of the chaos.

Margaret applies the lessons that scientists are learning from their study of nature to business organizations. We, as leaders, are a part of the very nature that scientists study. What can happen when we, as leaders in organizations, seek order, seek all the information? Applying the inverse of chaos theory, chaos emerges. In other words, Margaret reminds us that life seeks what works, not what is the perfect solution. How much time, ego, energy and certainty do we invest—if it's not perfect, we don't want our names attached!

This bit of coaching advice to the perfectionists among us is important. There have been a few leader participants I have met who are, by self-admission, perfectionists. The feedback trail throughout their surveys often indicates a tale of frustration and less motivation among their respondents. Additionally, their respondents often don't feel mutual trust, under a continuing questioning by the participant of their efforts and work, and little, if any, subsequent creativity, life, innovation and risk taking.

Fitting in well here is the previous role model's comment:

"We are either moving forward or backward, but we are not standing still."

The concluding comment

This final quote, tied to a role model "risk taker," embodies what others have called a philosophy of leadership through a stewardship mentality, as opposed to leadership through an entitlement mentality. If you are seeking an example reflecting a steward's mentality, the following comment serves that purpose.

"When I ask, 'Can you find this out for me?' I always consider whether I wasted that person's time. I usually go with a gut call when I have approximately 80 percent of the information, because the other 20 percent is just too costly to seek and a waste of mine, and importantly, others', time."

Here, this leader's behavior is not suggesting a mentality of entitlement. The leader is not requiring the time of his people without thought to these people's needs and priorities. Would to do otherwise contribute to an appearance of the leader as being entitled by virtue of his position? Rather, this role model's thinking and actions reflect an appearance of the leader as serving and respecting people's needs and priorities. How does the perfectionist tend to appear to others, as entitled or as steward? How do you appear to others, as entitled or as steward? Do we have a choice as to how we create our appearance to others in the future? Which appearance better serves us on our journey toward realizing and producing meaning in life—as steward or as entitled?

Again, notice the overlap of actions, wisdom and philosophy as the voice of role models for business, for productivity and making money, speak to us in the next chapter.

4

Business

"It's a company office, not my office. They are our people, not my people. I'm a steward—it's not mine."

- Participant

Are you looking for ways to leverage the sister behaviors within the visionary and risk taking categories? Based on what role model leaders for business-focused behaviors indicate, making money and productivity are direct beneficiaries of those previous two behavior groupings.

Business behaviors are about making money, creating value, productivity, reducing costs and exhibiting superior business judgment. Behaviors include: making appropriate business tradeoffs; demonstrating the ability to increase both making money and cost savings; improving productivity; meeting all financial targets; negotiating effectively; and taking actions resulting in increased business and client success.

When considering all the business behaviors collectively, I, again, noticed a definitive pattern of reoccurring responses from leaders in varying environments, and at different levels of leadership.

The pattern sounded like this: "Marty, I'm always asking questions of my people relative to the business."

In some cases, it is especially important to note what hierarchical level of leadership the specific leader occupies. This next participant statement comes from a team leader who had no real financial responsibility among her position requirements as of yet. When other team leaders, who were her peers, received their feedback, their respondents generally marked *not applicable* or *not observed* for these same business behaviors. Yet employees, or directs, of this particular leader, were not only marking some opinion of frequency in the business behaviors, they were marking "always" and "role model" for frequency!

> "Marty, I'm always asking questions of my people, especially my technical people, questions like: 'When choosing between solution (a) and (b), does one of them have a better chance of reducing costs eight months down the road?'"

Her point was that the employees might ask, "What's significant about eight months from now?" Or they may refer back to the broader business backdrop against which they are making specific decisions and choices.

Another similar example occurred with a call center supervisor. Like his fellow supervisors, he had no real financial responsibility. Unlike his fellow supervisors, he received opinions from his respondents on the business behaviors, and those opinions of frequency were at the role model marking. To the question, "What do you do...?" he replied, "I tend to ask questions of my people to get them to think about the business reasons for decisions made at a higher level. For example, my team was grumbling because each person's quota of number of calls per month had been increased. I asked them how many total calls per month were they being asked to increase? How many total people in the call center took calls in a month's time? Then I asked them for the sum of the total calls that month. What would cause our client to make this kind of request? As they talked, they realized benefits of taking on more calls and became more aware of some larger business issues."

One leader had switched from a line to a staff job position. His entire career had been on the client-facing, revenue-generating account. Now, he was serving in an internal corporate staff position. He had chosen his respondents for his feedback from his current role, so they, too, were serving in roles that were not directly generating revenue. He was surprised to see that all of his respondents had opinions for the business behaviors in the report and that they were also marking "role model" for frequency. He responded, "Marty, all I can figure is that I'm the one who is always asking questions, especially of my peers, like, 'If we were in the business of making money here, where's the money maker in these choices? What would we choose to do here if we were the client-facing account? (or) What happens if we don't spend the money here? (or) Where can we get the biggest bang for our buck here? (or) If you were paying the overhead, what would you want to pay us for?' In asking people questions like these, it increases their awareness, at their own level. They think and act more broadly."

One theme that I captured from the business behavior role models was the habit of incorporating the business aspects of work life naturally into their communication, as if it was normal everyday conversation. It made me realize the advantage of talking business in little ways over time, as opposed to the occasionally big, concentrated shotgun approach to communicating a lot of business for a brief time, then giving it no lip service until a later date. Otherwise stated, out of sight, out of mind.

Note this following person's rationale for the high perception of his feedback among the business behaviors: "I'm always including references to business within my normal conversations, such that it is given routine attention in all thinking and decisions by every team member. I may be asking how their child's soccer game was the night before and, in the next breath, could be saying, 'Do you know who is paying for this?'"

A similar expression of this theme can be drawn from this comment: "I inherited a group of people who did not have a clue about the contracts they were working under. So, I copied the contracts, distributed them to each person and, after some familiarization and discussion, tested them and gave them chocolates for the right answers. Marty, it's a year later now and they're ahead of me. They know when they're in scope and out of scope (of the work as defined by the contract). They're making suggestions to the client executive directly, and when they're doing something extra at the request of the customer that is beyond scope, they are already letting the customer know that early on. They see ways to build onto our business, and we've actually signed some add-on business as a result. They tell me how different their conversations with each other and the customer have become compared to how they used to sound before my time."

Yet another leader in a totally different environment made the same conclusion. "I review the contract with every person on the account, quiz them and give them prizes for correct answers. They input what they are obligated to provide and determine our expense, billing and other financial information. They look for how and where to save money, and they get 10 percent of every saving."

One leader emphasized the importance of incorporating business into job performance feedback. "I evaluate my directs (people working directly for me) using the language of the contract. 'What are you doing that makes money?'"

As influenced by the wording of a particular business behavior statement, many comments from the role models included the advantage of discussing tradeoffs in conversation. Notice the following pattern from an assortment of different leaders.

"Seeing the tradeoffs convert into dollars and cents, reference productivity, revenues, etc. We are not making that association if decisions are based on good technical considerations alone. We clarify what's intuitive, what's direct, what's implicit and what's explicit."

"Whether they know it or not, everyone weighs the pros and cons, even at a subconscious level. So communicate in such a way that the good outweighs the bad."

70

"Tradeoffs - we work issues from both sides, the business problem, and technical capability. Choosing which battles is a matter of perspective."

"We brainstorm tradeoffs, accumulate ideas, establish realistic goals and target dates, or else it all becomes frustrating and low in priority."

"Considering tradeoffs is a matter of asking key questions and turning responses into actions. It's not needing or requiring perfect information. It's quickly weighing the risk versus the benefits ratio and the rewards. How much does it cost to not have perfect information compared to the cost of having perfect information?"

"Tradeoffs are alternatives."

"It's asking, 'What problem would you rather live with?'"

"I discuss the business sense with people. For example, ask questions like, 'What happens if we/they do not spend the money? What's the tradeoff?'"

"When considering tradeoffs, consider that revenue is a function of customer satisfaction, which is a function of delivery, which is a function of people."

"It's coming to the table with multiple alternatives, weighing the roles and deciding which ones to choose. In larger meetings, establishing and using criteria, and weighting these criteria, leads people to thinking. Asking the right people the right questions collaboratively gets them involved."

"The tradeoff is reasonableness versus a sense of urgency. It's a function of priority and the issue.

The higher the stakes, the more time for sanity checks, so timeliness varies. I frame the key issues, how much time, how good a decision model needed, say 80/20."

"Thinking through tradeoffs mean exercising judgment and gathering those that agree or disagree, and their rationale."

"Tradeoffs are contingency planning. We have a daily triage meeting. We prioritize, which influences our future work. Emergencies are classified as either routine, contractual or as posing a media liability. Where are the costs?"

"An example of communicating tradeoffs is telling the customer you can do that, but the ramifications are (a), (b) and (c)."

"Value is focused on the long term. Price is focused on the short term. That's a tradeoff."

"Implementing change and leveraging diversity is all about discussing and openly communicating tradeoffs in daily decisions, small and large."

As you continue to read over other business behavior role model comments, notice the themes emerging out of their responses.

"Engineers like the bells and whistles. Yet they respond to recovering expenses. 'If we can't fund this within the project, we have to recover costs elsewhere, so help me build the business case.' They go from a huge Christmas list down to a small needs list."

I say to my customer, 'Are we being paid to do this? Should we be doing this work? I've identified what I do for you (the customer) that you don't pay me to do.' They appreciate and respect that."

"We use results-oriented objectives. Not objectives saying, 'Be productive,' but saying, 'Eliminate costs for our client.'"

"Reactive reacts to a business reduction, and proactive grows the business. It's a Blinding Flash of the Obvious (BFO)."

"Our proposals must answer the question, 'What will it do for you? Will this convince you to pay the price?'"

"I have to buy in myself, believe in what we are doing myself, before convincing others. When we believe it ourselves, we accept accountability. If not, we play the victim."

"I was assigned to take over the money and financials from my peers. However, I kept them in the loop, and that, apparently, promoted respect."

"Positioning the business is a function of training the people."

"I keep leaders and others informed with charts and other visible communications. I keep people off the bench, off from being in a non-billable status. I anticipate the end of a project by promoting them in advance to other executives for another project."

"I see peers as my friends. Their problems are my problems."

"I talk to my people about getting outside the nine dots. If you could do this, you'd be saving us money."

"Understanding motivating factors behind an issue—they (the client) want one year, we want a perpetual contract. What's a factor behind their want? It's an ability to control price. We go from there."

"I'm always asking my people questions like, 'What are you doing that generates revenue? (or) What are you doing to take the application to the next level, the next level of support? What are you doing to Web-enable your service?'"

"I give feedback to my people on our customer's needs and where we provide value. Value is how does it make things better?"

"An example of leveraging resources and leveraging the big picture to save money and achieve a win-win: A vendor bids on my $15 million of business and is willing to discount thirty cents to the dollar for service, instead of bidding on each of $1 million dollars over fifteen different business units, and gives me only ten cents to the dollar discount. Is it a tradeoff? Yes. Perhaps service is a little less tailored to specific units' needs, but the overall benefit and value outweighs the complete customization for every unit. It's not just what is the best solution at our level, but from end to end, so we engage more people."

"I talk money all the time with my people. I share the targets, talk the language, for their learning and understanding."

"I sell the new initiative, by giving them time to buy in. That's done through asking questions—for example, 'What do we need to do this?' I allow some venting, then get to a 'We will do this' phase, and attack with vigor and enthusiasm."

"It's phasing over time *from* control first (documenting business processes, desktop procedures, who you contact, meetings, etc.) *to* having time to pursue growth."

"I use analogies to help people think about business decisions they make. For example, what costs/services to cut and not to cut—my kids' going to college is an investment, it's not, 'Don't go to college, I'm cutting costs.'"

"An expense report is a financial decision."

"I look for simplification and am not quick to be constrained by perceived boundaries—what's the question; what's the problem; do we really understand?"

"It is asking questions to promote people's business thinking. For example, we're running a company on spreadsheets and PowerPoint presentations. In these presentations, the presenter might say we're saving X amount of money. I'll ask, 'Did you? OK, who's P&L (Profit and Loss balance statement), who's outlook did it come out of?' No one can answer, so we're not there, it's smoke and screen. Yes, it's valuable work, but how are we measuring? Or at least, will the owner of the financials agree? Often, the presenters haven't even talked with that owner."

"An example of conflict turned into a partnership—sales and delivery now operate as a virtual team. Sales engage in a role early with us. Formerly, we saw them just trying to make us (in delivery) work harder. Partnership and ownership has turned them into us, us into them. We partly achieved this by asking questions like, 'How do we complement one another?'"

"Making money includes I'll accept a lot of work and share where we stand with people."

"The best technical solution is not necessarily the best business solution."

"I identified subject matter experts among my directs and gave each of them one of six contracts. They monitor, learn, update the team. I eventually get them to write the RFPs (Request for Proposals). They are always following up with the customer."

This next leader was also very high in the strategic/visionary thinking behaviors. This is an example of how that strength had an impact in their account, both making money and experiencing a consistent increase in business compared to other accounts.

"I had to orient my people away from a stability and predictability mentality to a stability and growth mentality. Stability and predictability became a wall for them, and they had become stuck there."

"We used to talk in terms of scope—we can't or don't do that for the customer. Now, it's who talks contract, who talks delivery to the customer. We now focus on what we can do, not what we can't do for the customer."

"From more selling price to selling value."

"All of my people's objectives tie to generating income. How can we package our most successful projects?"

"Important thing about a loss is to not lose the lesson. Remember the lesson."

"We discuss things like tradeoffs. Our revenue is the client's expense, and the client's expense impacts their profitability. So a win-win becomes us considering their problems too. They have to cut costs, we have to increase revenues, which becomes a dilemma. Yet a win-win example is a way to do both. The customer helps me find non-traditional business, and I help the customer cut costs."

"It's about explaining the context, the big picture business reasons, not just telling them."

"I'm realistic, and you can't get mad about reality. Focus not on what I don't have, rather focus on what I do have."

"All my directs understand the financial business, so they understand how they impact, and even more, they communicate with clients at their level, to seize on the notion and communicate, 'Here's the added value we do for you.'"

Educational background

I noticed that those leaders with a financial or business-oriented college degree and those without that specific business educational background shared common behavioral examples as their reasoning for being perceived so highly. Certainly, those leaders having an education in business or finance, and willing to communicate and talk business in everyday language with others, had an advantage here. Yet, regardless of educational level, or major, they all shared a common thread of asking questions and showing a desire to engage in inquisitive and thought-provoking conversations with all of their respondents. This, in turn, seemed to generate a degree of comfort among their respondents about talking business with one another.

Another common trait was the desire and willingness to share financial information that other leaders, who were marked lower, seemed to lack. The philosophy of leaders lower in the business specific behaviors indicated some apprehension to sharing too much of the financial information at the risk of losing some competitive advantage. This included leaders with an educational background in finance. It typically included a broader issue of trust.

However, I noticed one differentiator among those with a financial background, compared to those without. The leaders with a financial degree or background seemed to more often have evidence of business obvious to the naked eye if you were to walk into their office. They would typically be the ones to say, "See, Marty," and point to their walls, covered with non-confidential financial data spreadsheets. If someone walked in, be it their client, leader, employee or peer, they could engage them in a conversation by looking right at the wall, and not be limited to having to view looking over some binder of presentation foils.

Sharing of information in little ways every day, invoking a spirit that everyone, regardless of role, is a business person, commonly marked the pathway of business role model leaders, regardless of the business environment or the country.

As we'll see, these traits also served as a foundation for business negotiations and for resolving conflict.

5

Negotiations and Resolving Conflict

"I do not initially say 'No' to my customer, but 'Let me see.' Then, should I come back 'No,' they usually don't even question it."

- Participant

When relating with people coming from a variety of perspectives, of preferred styles of communicating, and of different approaches to life, disagreements and conflicts become part of the landscape. Although negotiating with a client does not automatically infer one is resolving a conflict, the role model leaders for behaviors pertaining to resolving conflict and to negotiating a win-win effectively, give overlapping responses and examples for both. As you will see, the first comment chosen below from a role model leader reveals that from experience, "Our clients tend to make requests for service with a predetermined path in their mind more often than the desired end point or destination." You can usually generalize by substituting any individual or group of people for the word "client" and that statement still applies. This awareness, alone, should begin to accelerate your better understanding the request of another, be they spouse, child, teacher, neighbor or employee, through clarification and listening.

This chapter describes some of the thinking, tips and techniques that role model leaders use in negotiations and resolving conflict. Some also identify sample ways to both give and make promises and requests.

Some would suggest that it is not an overgeneralization to say all conversations are, in essence, a form of negotiating. With that in mind, consider this a supplementary chapter on communicating.

We'll begin with a series of client-focused responses from role model leaders, with some insights on how they approach negotiations and resolving conflict.

Client-focused insights

While coming from three different leaders, notice the commonality in all three sets of comments that immediately follow. They speak a common language and demonstrate some approaches for receiving customer or client complaints.

> "Our clients tend to make requests (for service) with a predetermined path in their mind more often than the desired end point or destination. So I put myself in the customer's place, understanding their mindset, expectations and concerns. For example, the client might say—'You guys aren't servicing me.' I'll ask, 'What did you ask them to do? What did you want them to do? What were you really trying to accomplish?'"

> "Customer complaints are based on a cost to their business, and their own emotion. You handle both."

> "It starts with understanding the customer's language. I feel their pain. Their work stops if they have no PC (personal computer)."

While the next comment is from one leader, I had heard numerous responses with the same familiar ring that this one provides.

"When an upset person approaches me, because a customer has screamed at them, I'll first say something like, 'I see what you mean; you must feel so low. What a shame.' I'll listen and empathize to that effect. Then I'll sense when it's time, and secondly, ask them questions and have conversation around possible customer motive. 'What do you think would cause the customer to shout like that? What kind of pressures or tension is the customer experiencing? Have you ever experienced doing that yourself?' Thirdly, I'll offer alternatives, and ask something like, 'What do you want? Would you like me to talk with the customer? Do you want to talk with the customer? Do you want both of us? Or do you want to let it go for now?' Usually they want to handle it themselves, and feel better prepared after our conversation. I might even briefly role-play with them to experience how that conversation might sound, and increase their comfort level and confidence through preparation."

Other role model comments include these:

"Deal with difficult customers by (1) listening to all points of view; (2) seek and do a win-win—WIIFM, (what's in it for me), and WIIFY (what's in it for you), not all or nothing. Sometimes it's not about money; it's about pride. You can give without really giving anything (of substance). I never brought contract into a conversation with my customer. If needed, I give an issue to my contract people. It's not personal, and you do not insult their intelligence. Positions are negotiated. You cannot cure everything in life; you can only manage relationships. For instance, how do you deal with a screamer? I can't change or cure that, but I can negotiate—what does the screamer want, while pounding their fist. I can give you this, not that. You negotiate, based on your leverage, and you resolve it. Contracts haven't resolved anything. Business, in the end, is a people business. Do I want to do business with you? Smart people know it's a win-win."

"Crisis requires constant, immediate feedback with the client, even if it's just, 'Here's what we've done. I don't have an answer yet.'"

"Initially, I subordinate myself to the client's needs. I'm somewhat quiet, asking questions, listening as the relationship matures. Then, I gradually increase my dialogue. I become more of a peer, challenge them, and share the bigger picture."

"The client may have an agenda—personal or business—you don't understand. So develop a relationship with the client that is a little broad, a little deep, so you can provide checks and balances with your company's reputation and have up-front, candid conversations on a regular basis."

"When negotiating, I always ask myself, and preach, 'What is this person thinking? If they are sitting here, what are they hearing? Orient our issues and resolution with their thinking, seeing alternatives. Understand others' behavior, not to agree, but to figure out how to respond, how to plan strategy."

"Getting to yes is getting to the common ground, the level playing field. We live in language."

"Our customer's bonus is partly based on what they save and get out of our hide. I'll anticipate, on an occasion, and say to my customer, 'OK, you know what's true, but this time, I'll eat it. Now, you owe me."

"I help people to think more clearly in a crisis situation. If the customer or some leader is yelling at you or hard on you, I sit down with you, and say, 'If the system doesn't work, who will die?' It's a matter of perspective."

"If necessary, ask everybody else to leave. Just you and I sit and talk. It's convincing the person that you're there for them to succeed. Walk away if you have to, to be firm."

"Too many people argue a position instead of a point." (Arguing a position breeds becoming inflexible, unbending, not listening, and eventually results in losing.)

"If you give something away and you get nothing in return later, then (1) it's of no value to you, and (2) you create a culture of entitlement. Customer says, you should be giving to me, versus the customer thinking they'll do something for me in return as well."

"People do business with whom they like. Seek the relationship first, then the capabilities second. People buy on relationships. Be responsive, return their calls. We're not a product business, not even a service business, because most of what we do is a commodity."

"When negotiating, I'm thinking, 'If I change this, or did not give in on that one, how would that affect the outcome?'"

"Client relations, resolving conflicts and negotiating is as much about relationship as it is solution driven. You can have the best solution, say characterized by ease of implementation. If the solution is not in the budget, it gets no airtime, regardless of the payback. But relationship means you are thinking down the same path with your customer or client. So understanding where they want to go, offering something they'd really be interested in, is the by-product of a good client relationship."

"Initially I ask the client, 'What is it you most want to have happen? How can I support you?' To conclude, I always ask the client: 'Is there any question I should have asked?' This engages people." (This participant indicated that this series of questions was especially valuable when meeting a potentially new customer or client.)

General insights

Here's what the role model leaders say in general about negotiations and resolving conflict beyond a client interaction.

"I anticipate and pull a person aside. I take anything bad and spin it into a flip side positive at the conclusion. I'm saying, 'Watch for this. Keep doing that.'"

"I'll first say, 'What do you want from me—to listen and be a sounding board? To offer advice? To talk to the other party with you, or for you?'"

"It's what you do after the conflict—all people have different ways of dealing with conflict. How you approach them later is the differentiator. From 'no grudges, not personal' to 'appreciated.' This takes being objective."

"I remind my folks that unflattering comments from our client are just as welcome. So let's do something about it—help them feel special."

"When handling conflict, focus on the behavior or focus on the message."

"My tone of voice remains calm, sounding like a priest in the confessional."

"You cannot dictate a solution to a conflict."

"Self-centered means holding onto your anger and prizing it as if it gives you an edge (over others). Bitterness only consumes the vessel containing it."

"I think to myself, 'What's your pain?' It's my pain, but when I see pain in others, we see ourselves, see our sameness in others. We share in the human condition. Pain can captivate us and make us become self-absorbed. We withdraw. Instead, use pain to help us, to make us stronger."

"I anticipate obstacles and promote proactive planning. With these possible scenarios, do you have some mitigation activities?"

"Before saying no, I'll try to (1) negotiate ('Can you do this part? I'll do that part.'); (2) delegate it to another, if possible; or (3) renegotiate the timeline, and do that against a backdrop of my task organizer, tracking out at least six months."

"We don't mean or need consensus as unanimous. No! Consensus means all have been heard and considered."

"I help translate the bitches of others into actionable suggestions to those targeted by the bitching."

"I sponge an argument in conversation. 'I heard you. You already said that.' Then the argument is not going anywhere but into the sponge, to defuse the argument. Deflect arguments back to the task or rule under discussion. For example, 'That may be; nonetheless, do your homework (or) wash the dishes.'"

"Conflict resolution is about getting them to see another's viewpoint."

I was reminded of this previous participant's comment when listening to a sermon at church one day. The priest was referring to a reading in the Book of Wisdom and said one definition of wisdom is developing the capacity to see another's view different from your own. If this definition of wisdom is of benefit to you, then you can say that practicing the skill of resolving conflict is also practicing a kind of human wisdom!

"If we just argue, it becomes productive for neither of us. Let's return and revisit this when ready, so we can reach a decision."

"Always blaming people results in lowered trust from others...less collaborative activity. Being abrasive prevents others from seeing your values, your contributions."

"What would you do if you were me?"

"I'll ask them to document, write it down first, which usually begins to settle them down before we talk it over."

"When people vent in the heat of the moment, it is not representative of how they feel at the end of the day. Filter, have perspective, remain grudge free with employees and customers."

"I saw a model used once which indicated that a way of having more choices is to increase a space between the impulses we feel and our reaction or response to those impulses. So, when someone cuts me off the road while I'm driving the car and I angrily respond, my brain is so powerful, so quick to react, it's like which happened first—my being cut off, or my reaction to it? I can't control these impulses that occur in life. These impulses will always occur, usually when I least expect it. What I can control, however, is my response or reaction to those impulses. I found application of this model at work when resolving conflict, and I use it to coach others. So at work, the question becomes, 'How do I increase a space between impulses I experience and my reaction to them?' If someone cuts me off in conversation or calls me a jerk out loud in front of others, I have choices. I can choose the fight response and call them a name back (and escalate the situation). I can choose flight response, thinking that if we're in front of customers, it is better to withhold my tongue. Or I can choose some other alternative. How do I get to that point of having other alternative choices—not because fight or flight is wrong. Either one of those may be an appropriate choice in a given situation. How do I get to a point of having other choices? Going back to the idea our brains are so powerful, I can ask myself the question in my mind, 'What is it I really want to say right now?' Even if I respond to the rude comment at work by beginning to respond, 'What I most want to say is...' that may be all the added space I need between the impulse I experienced when called a jerk and having more choices from which to respond to that impulse. For example, I now might choose to respond, 'What I most want to say is, I feel the tension rising within me when I hear you say that, but I know your heart is in the right place. Help me understand better. What did you notice that caused you to say that?'"

"I disagree without becoming disagreeable."

"I hold one-on-one conversations, talk at the level of perceptions, not about the actions themselves, to get people to see the other side. First step in surfacing the problem, before resolving: 'Have you ever told someone their behavior drives you crazy?' One example of perception was that which my client had of one of my employees. They saw him as a lazy worker. He actually arrived an hour before everyone else, because he dropped his wife off for work at another location. He arrived at his desk at 7:15 (a.m.), read the morning newspaper, drank coffee until 7:45 (a.m.), then started working fifteen minutes early, since he wasn't scheduled to start until 8:00 (a.m.). Perceived by the client as a lazy worker, this employee was actually a hard worker."

"In some extremes, I've taken the visual away by causing people to talk sitting back to back."

"If a person is not secure with themselves, then they are not honest with themselves and are not confident about who they are. So a dysfunction of always trying to fix another (as if their parent), to fix another person, to make them better behaved, or less sick, is to establish a co-dependency, a need to control other people, so as to feel secure about themselves. If truly secure with themselves, then they are not so quick to act out irrationally, not so quick to lash out at others, to get upset when others make a mistake, or when they don't meet their expectations when they want them met. If insecure, anger is directed towards blaming people, not blaming the problem or error. However, if confident in who they are, they accept others as they are and do not try to make them conform to their mood. The person always talking, always at the center of attention, lacks security. The more humble they are, the more secure. If I don't feel good inside me, I do cause others to react, meaning I'm controlling. So if you are growing, you have a need to prove to others. If you are grown, no need to prove. These are the kinds of conversations I have with people to understand their conflicts with others and their part in them."

"When people are trying to understand the motive, or what happened to cause the reaction, I get them to think about what happened right before the reaction."

"My strategy is that I expect them to challenge me. I see that as a positive, not a negative. Then I can challenge them."

"I do what I call an examination of discovery. First, what can we agree on? Second, OK, what remains are the differences. Third, what are issues around these differences? And fourth, can we live with these...?"

"I use the analogy with people that constant conflict suggests that people are in a state of *dis*-ease, which health care specialists indicate that upwards of 90 percent of our diseases are caused by stress, or by being in a constant state of *dis*-ease. This provides a perspective and motivation to rise above petty conflict."

"Escalating tension affects rational thought."

"They're mad at situations, not at you."

"In a worst-case scenario, I'm asking the person a question like, 'OK, if there are these ten things that bug you about this person, what is one thing that you like? How can you use that one thing to rebuild your relationship? (Or if there is none) OK, tell me one thing you have in common with that person (for example, you both smoke). Can you use that opportunity to share more?' From that social interaction, it already begins to take less effort."

"Do you think you'll remember this conversation in five years? Is anyone in the hospital as a result? (Example of setting perspective) A little humor helps. Do we want to fight this battle, or creatively divert?"

"I can really get mad, or I can say, 'What if there's something to this? What could I do to apply that awareness? Everyone can always improve.'"

"I'll get people to appreciate each other, very positive, we're in this together. An overall leader, or client leader, as a screamer, creates finger-pointing layers below. This diffuses energy and the productive capacity of larger teams. You must separate the emotional side and work through it objectively. What are the facts of the issue? This goes beyond who said what. Begin with the end in mind, and let people decompress. Then ask, 'When was the deliverable due? When's the client expecting it? What are the requirements not met?'" (This can be applied in non-business scenarios also.)

"In conflict, I speak positively, constructively, in a way that people want to change, that people see what's in their best interests. Communicate options, alternatives, tradeoffs, and the relative good in each, versus communicating specifically what to do."

"Observe emotions first. What are the emotions? Then, what are the facts behind it? I'll say, 'Help me understand…(how) they come to their own conclusions.'"

"People react the same emotionally to problems, whether the computer shuts down or a relative causes the upset."

"Putting data on a board where people can see, then the tone changes."

"It's how one is **after** the conflict."

Notice the wisdom within the seven words of the previous comment? This participant credited behaving by taking the high road following the conflict or disagreement, for being called a role model for resolving conflict. Can you recall previous confrontations when, after the encounter, how you thought and what you conveyed in communication, both verbally and nonverbally, affected the situation moving forward? Do your facial expressions and nonverbal demeanor contribute to the relationship continuing within the tone and memory of that conflict? Or do you contribute to the relationship moving forward beyond the conflict? What occurs after the conflict can have even more importance in determining the health of the relationship going forward. Conflicts give us a continuing opportunity to display the essence of our humanity.

Asking people questions, not getting ourselves wrapped into the emotions of the moment, wanting to first understand others, looking beyond others' emotions, are among the hallmarks of leaders in negotiations and resolving conflicts. Are these an extension of what role model leaders do who are recognized for maintaining client-focused behaviors and excellent relationships with their client?

6

Client Focused

People do business with whom they like. Sell the relationship first, the capabilities second.
- Participant

This short chapter continues the theme that relationships start with the client is key, as noted by the role model leaders who negotiate and resolve conflict with those clients.

Behaviors include building and maintaining client relationships and creating value and profit for the client.

These first comments reinforce the notion that leaders just don't do it on their own. This next one particularly showcases some coaching that a higher-level leader does with the larger organization.

"I'll ask 'Who's your client?' If I call that client and said, 'Is so and so adding value?' Would they know about that person? If not, then we haven't connected and we aren't doing our job."

"I have redefined who the clients are with my team. Not as the end client, but whomever you are

93

supporting. Whoever impacts our client in the end, either in cost or delivery, is our client too."

"To promote increased relationships with the client among our organization and learn, I'll ask, 'If we turn off the service, what will that do to the relationship with the client?' Ask the client, 'Tell me how your business works'. I may look stupid, but I appear very interested."

"You lessen the perception with more data points. What's your customer's perspective, if that is yours? Ask from the customer's view, why would I pay for that? And ask the inverse of the questions. Would I allow my company to give you substandard service?"

"I play back what I hear in a way that's seen as adding value."

"Key on how what we are doing ties to the client's business and organizational objectives. Have something to further their agendas, beyond the business."

"When we mess up, be urgent for the customer. What do I expect when I walk into a dealership with a broken car for a second time? That they escalate to the head mechanic."

That previous comment presents timeless advice. When, in our lifetime, have we acted out the part of the upset customer? When have we experienced an unpleasant, unresponsive service provider?

To take advantage of this timeless quality is to put us in our customer's shoes. Can you put yourself in their shoes, having been in similar shoes, in a similar position yourself?

"We have to know what pains the customer. Know what the customer rewards us for."

"Clients look at risk from a business point of view, not a technical point of view. We need to ask, is technological innovation of benefit to the client?"

"Always leave something positive with the customer—a new insight, an interesting article, leave something with them."

"I never see myself as a salesman going to the customer. I ask to understand their issues, maybe describe to them why the Internet is important, how security is important. They don't hear our company's name in those things, they hear issues important to them, they hear this is what we've done, what we can't do, what things they should be thinking about. They eventually ask me, 'Can our company do this, and can you help us here?' Otherwise, they can sense if I'm just trying to sell when I come in as the salesperson."

That point about how not seeing self as a salesperson when meeting the customer or client was a pattern of response I heard from those who succeed with their clients. How do you see yourself when you visit or call on your client?

7

People Care—Coaching, Team Orientation, Communicating and Sharing the Knowledge

Taking ourselves too seriously is a function of valuing the task. Taking things or ourselves less seriously is a function of valuing the relationship, more time with people.

- Participant

To break down people care any further than what this chapter title indicates would dilute the powerful message of people care. What do perceived role model leaders who care for people, individually and as a team, claim they do or say to create role model perceptions? What do they accomplish? When you think of people for whom you have worked who were strong communicators, leaders who took a strong interest in people, the team, and in sharing knowledge, what do you recall them doing? As you review the following behaviors, note to yourself what you recall the best in practice doing, and then compare with the pattern of responses below. Which of their practices might you incorporate more regularly into your own behaviors? Which of these do you realize you do, but only occasionally, as opposed to daily?

Sharing the knowledge, leveraging information, learning, coaching and communicating fit like gloves to one another when listening to the role models describe their actions. Behaviors include sharing and facilitating information and learning; converting learning and knowledge into growth; and developing others through effective coaching and mentoring. Communicating and displaying a team orientation are addressed later in this chapter.

Coaching

Listening to the role model coaches, the repetitive familiarity of these two primary responses resounds like a broken record in my memory.

First was availability or accessibility. "Marty, it's not like I'm so busy that people just feel so guilty for seeking me out. Even when my door is open and, say, I'm on the phone, I still notice a presence, a shadow by my door, and always, with a welcoming smile, nonverbally either wave them on in or gesture that I will find them."

Second, listening. These leaders continually comment on their ability to listen and its essential importance in coaching. "Marty, I've often heard feedback describing me as a listener, as one who wears the other person's shoes in conversation."

Notice the similarities in messages as you think about the comments of role model coaches.

> "The leader too busy to coach is like the second of two people chopping wood in a race. One stops every hour to sharpen the saw, the second keeps on chopping. The one who stops every hour wins."

> "I communicate and listen 'gently.' It's how you say it. It's spoken in your tone, mannerisms, even when overwhelmed. Apologize readily. 'I blew it.' Question for the deeper understanding, the deeper issues, and use follow-up questions."

"Need to connect; I'm changing too, trying to understand them versus influence them. It's not as if I'm going to change them."

"I'm always sharing what I know, training people to replace me."

"If people are told to take this number of classes by this date and people are putting them off until the last minute, then ask, 'Are we attending to develop, or are we attending to meet a requirement? Are we developing for the sake of measuring, or for checking, or for development?'" (Discussion on measurement and development)

"I ask myself and others, 'What can I do in little ways, over time, to help you realize fulfillment of what's most important to you in your life, through your work?'"

"I make myself available and accessible, and show an interest in what they're doing. I allow people to vent and ask questions. I'll ask questions like, 'When do you think that change occurred?'"

"Deming (Dr. W. Edwards Deming, a recognized quality master and consultant on statistical studies) talked about rekindling that desire and fire for learning, despite grades. Even promoting a hobby from outside of work, and bringing that different perspective into the workplace, becomes value."

"I went **from** if I'm not coding, if I'm not getting work done, I'm not productive, **to** if I'm facilitating and coaching, I am productive."

"I'm told the performance reviews I give contain lots of feedback. Messages like, 'Let's get you in some task forces to push the business.' What holds people back is that others won't tell them the little things. That's the difference between a good and great performance review."

"It's efficiency versus effectiveness. I opt for effectiveness for a higher purpose—availability. My printer is on the other side of the hall, not in my office. I'm making myself available for people to talk with."

"It's not the image of the athletic coach screaming from the sidelines. It's more as a coach/quarterback, being on the playing field with them."

"When coaching someone in conflict or disagreement with another, first match and then lead their behavior. Understand their perspective first, and get them comfortable. Not contradicting them or disagreeing outright initially, just reflecting their concerns. Eventually, go to asking questions such as, 'How do you think the person feels?' Then go to leading the conversation."

"I get people to see learning as generative, with an eye towards where each experience is taking you. There's something to be learned from not being selected. For every door that shuts, another opens."

(Same leader from above continues) "I'm asking how can I support you, how can I help you? It's in the one-on-ones, not the annual performance review. I use coaching questions to promote understanding learning as generative, such as: 'What made you do this? What specific experience most impacted your choice, or most impacted your taking this path?'"

"I always end with the last thing asked, 'Is there something I can do for you, or that you need from me?'"

"I might say, 'Let's put all this data aside for now. What problem are we really trying to solve?'"

"A mistake that is negative is positive when learning is realized."

"I often ask, 'Everybody understand what that means?'"

"I remind people of our goals. When taking our mind off our goals, our mind tends to see obstacles and gravitate to what is frightful."

"I bring the class to them, make it real to what they're doing."

"I coach open-mindedness, so it comes from a position of surrender, learning, self-confidence and curiosity. This helps my leaders to become good in delegating authority. The opposite is closed mindedness. Then you come from a position of shutdown, a defensive posture such as, 'I'm right;' a needing to feel right, validated and secure in who you are. So a different, new idea appears as a threat, so you then reject the thinking by speaking louder. This leads to micromanagement."

"What is it you most want to have happen? How can I support you?"

"I coach from a position of curiosity, not from a position of knowing. It's OK that I or you don't know, let's go figure it out."

"In a customer satisfaction review, my team used to focus on the 2 percent we did not do or get right. I've coached them now on focusing on the 98 percent we did get right. As a result, you can see the release of power and energy in the people."

"Listening without judgment is coaching without training."

"You can visit Pity City, you just can't move there."

"What can be right yesterday, may not work or be right today. There is a tendency for us to finger point and rip people apart."

"I help people see how what they do makes a difference. What they do matters. Ask, 'What is right about this? What is wrong?' Finish with the positive last; people remember leaving on a positive note. Recognize people's spirit more, less what their body is saying."

"One way to apply an environment of continuous learning is through 'coachable moments.' You get those by asking questions like, 'How could we have done this better?' And ask it again."

"It's being a force to support others in their development."

"I apply learning through coaching by relating simple analogies. For example, explaining risk management and issue management. A person is at risk when they are in the road and a car is approaching at 60 miles per hour. That's a risk. Later, I am lying on the road with tire tracks. I now have an issue, no longer a risk. Let's identify the risk before tire tracks appear on our face."

"You cannot force anyone when they are locked into a way of thinking that is very self-protective and self-gratifying. Show people how to find meaning and purpose in their life."

"If you show an interest in people, they'll work for you."

"There is more leverage focusing on and developing a person's strengths, than focusing on their weaknesses. So include and develop their strengths, and reap the rewards."

The following comment gives an example of a legacy that some leader out there left on another future leader, and generations of future employees, based on this role model's rationale.

"The reason for my being seen so high in coaching effectively started with my introduction to the company years ago. During my first formal leadership role, my leader focused me on coaching others. He said that is what leadership is about. Through the years since, that habit has continued, and it enables me to provide a balance between my people, the customer and the business."

Notice this leader continues to coach although he now has several teams and leaders reporting to him and has taken on more responsibility. He maintained the habit started in his first leadership role, taught to him by his first leader. He felt it was continuing to pay big dividends.

I also heard a number of participant comments specific to communicating expectations in a positive context, not in negative terms. I have heard there is a tendency for the brain to hear what not to do and do that very thing. So, as one participant put it, "Don't tell them to 'not fumble the ball,' because guess what they'll end up doing? Fumbling the ball! But rather, 'Hold on to the ball.'"

Another participant had me smiling and relating, recalling how mom used to say, "Don't trip," then they'd trip and mom would then say, often with hands on hips, "See, I told you not to trip." Or we might more accurately have heard it stated, "See, I told you you'd trip!"

Rather say, "Keep your footing; maintain your balance," anything except, "Don't trip!" (Despite that, moms were still the best.)

I was jogging on a track, when I overheard a parent soccer coach repeatedly exhorting young children. "Don't kick the ball high," he would coach. I thought to myself, here is a person I admire, totally committed, volunteering his time with our youth. And I recalled our quality master, Deming, in a seminar years earlier, commenting that despite people's best efforts, doing what we think is right, we can get farther away from what we really want to accomplish.

The message here for us is to listen to how we coach and direct others. Do we habitually use language that indicates what not to do, or do we use language that focuses people on what to do? As a further challenge for us who tend to speak in the negative, do we really know what it is we want to do in our own minds, or does speaking in the negative shadow our own confusion as to the team's purpose? This becomes an example of how we contribute to the very problems and issues with which we find ourselves consumed. This illustrates what some have stated in previous areas of leadership. The risk takers engage people to think about what's the worst that could happen. The visionaries guide people to always think about other possibilities. The motivator role models say the bottle is half full, not half empty, and focus on what is working before focusing on what is not working.

For the skeptics here, it's important to note that these same role model leaders professing half full do talk about lessons learned, what can improve and be done better. When you do so, do people feel life in your presence, or are they feeling something other than life? Are you generating confidence, with an associated increase in commitment, or are you breeding a lack of confidence and an associated reduction in the resolve, stake and confidence of others? What are you **choosing** to communicate daily, in little ways, over time? How is it affecting your reality each day? Regardless of how bad you perceive your leader to be, or how bad the environment, or how bad the relationship, or how bad the history, the ball is in your hands.

So, coaches, remember to give feedback in terms of **WHAT TO DO,** *NOT* **WHAT** *NOT* **TO DO.** It's not "Don't forget." It's "Remember!"

Communicating and sharing the knowledge

Communicating obviously occurs throughout this chapter, and the entire book. However, here are some ideas through the statements from role models more specific to communicating and sharing knowledge in the workplace. These behaviors include: demonstrates exceptional communication and listening; provides clear direction and timely feedback; shows a desire to discuss the views of others; actively shares information; and expresses self with perspective.

> "It's seeing how alternative motives to others' motives can free up or prevent attitudinal gridlock in self."

This previous comment reminds me of an attitude I had developed toward a high level leader over time. He was not located in my direct organization. My personal observation was that he was the type who would rain on your parade if he could. He would do so in conversation. His thinking was always negative, irritating, cross-examining, doubting and more. I had heard comments made by others toward him, as well, that reflected a similar opinion reinforcing my assessment. One day, I was invited into his leader's staff meeting. To begin their meeting, they first began with each person sharing anything that they wanted to, whether business or personal. When it came to his turn, this person shared some things that were occurring in his personal life that would challenge the stories of the biblical Job. As the meeting continued, I realized I was hearing him differently than I had previously. I paid special attention to the sense that he had not changed his tone or manner of speaking. It was how I was hearing him that had changed. What changed was my perspective of this person's motives. I saw alternative motives in this person that freed up my perspective that had been previously held in gridlock.

Other comments about communicating and sharing knowledge follow.

> "Before I write anything to be released, I determine (1) what are my key points; and (2) anticipate the reading audience's reaction, and their different experiences; then (3) I become prepared for a face-to-face. This leads to precise writing."

> "As a generalist, I create analogies from the various fields of engineering, financial, ergonomics, etc. My dad was a judge, so I learned to listen with empathy, listen the way they are listening, communicate the way they do, either street language or academically."

> "Ask yourself, what are they going to hear, NOT what are you going to say. 'We'll deliver in September.' Did they hear September 30th and you meant September 1st?"

> "The word 'why' sounds accusatory."

> "In communicating, be slow to anger and quick to forgive."

> "In a tough conversation, I'll start: 'This is hard for you to hear...not easy for me to say.' Then state the issue. For example, 'When you walk out of the

office, it prevents us working together. You're still doing these things.' You somehow relax; get people to listen, to share, employing empathy, sympathy and trust. I'll also use analogies. For example, take the subject of performance rankings. I'll say five students all score in the ninetieth percentile. If using one standard, all five students received an A. If using a curve, the person with a ninety is the lowest. They are walking out with an A minus score, not an A, B, C, D or F, which is a ranking score."

"I communicate my belief in their capacity, like the Pygmalion Effect." (Pygmalion Effect originates from Greek mythology. It infers that how you see a person determines how they behave. For instance, when you see a person as shy, they appear shy.)

"Ask the question differently when hearing the same responses."

"What do *we* need to do to get through this? It then becomes less of an issue to them. Just talking about it makes them feel better. They now have to articulate it, not just think about it. I might say, 'At this moment, I'm not happy about your performance, can we talk about it?' It's reciprocal. I can't fix, but can identify several alternatives."

"E-mail is OK, except for talking back and forth with a push back over an issue, then e-mail sounds tacky and becomes finger pointing. So follow up by phone. Otherwise, it becomes a huge round robin, downward spiral, and negative mode of communicating. Just like some corporate chat rooms. It's best not to reply by e-mail. Also, when I say 'corporate said,' that invites a defensive reaction among people. Now you have a bigger problem."

"Instead of saying, 'Here's what I heard,' I say, 'Here are some data points. How do they mesh into the information and situation you have?' That's the reason for having high clarity of communication."

"Our brains shut down when we hear, 'Yes, but...' Try saying it a little different like, 'Yes, and...' A small change, such as this, goes a long way."

"**'Why'** questions are to gain a historical perspective. When leading the conversation with **'what'** and **'how'** questions, it motivates the listener in subtle ways."

"The priority of communication is face to face, then phone, then, finally, leaving a voice mail, then e-mail. For voice mail and e-mail, limit your communication to bullet format information only."

"It is so important to understand how others perceive you, and how you can change that, and influence others accordingly."

"It's listening for clarity. If I don't hear accurately what was said, then it's unclear in my mind and I contribute to the ambiguity I complain about."

"I'll respond to different people's requests and needs immediately, as a matter of routine."

"Playing a variety of different roles helps me to ask the question."

"It's all in your delivery and choice of words. How you say things determines how people will react to you. I can say, 'Honey, when I look into your eyes, time stops.' Or I can say, 'Honey, when I look at you, I see a face that would stop a clock.' Same message, time stands still, yet in delivering, it's in our selection of the verbal and nonverbal."

"You can read your reflection off the expression of others."

"Good thoughts not spoken mean squat. The gift wasn't given."

"Instead of blaming, complaining or passing judgment on a direction, accept it, and communicate it factually to your teams."

"Responding to questions and seeing the light is having a *light bulb* moment, and increases confidence."

"I always follow up and communicate the value of the outcome to them."

"Listen to what I'm saying, not what words I'm speaking. What did you hear? What were your thoughts when you heard those words?"

"Asking 'why' implies doubting, questioning and disbelief."

"People generally prefer one-on-one conversation over e-mail. Pull everyone together, or in small groups. People want the verbal over the e-mail. We solicit others' ideas...results in developing a business case, and we present to management. For example, Internet access was eliminated, so we developed a business case for training, which requires firewall access. We developed a solution through people communicating together."

"An example of expressing patience is saying 'I might have done it this way,' versus finger pointing or 'You screwed up.'"

"When you say it, you own it."

"To say, 'Go do it, implement' is empowering. Inability to follow through does not empower."

"Listening *for* means being open to possibilities. Listening *about* means listening with historical, preordained assessments."

"I'm tuned in to everything. When I hear a person say, 'Whoa,' I'll ask, 'What made you react?' or I'll ask, 'What about this don't you understand?'"

"One-on-one conversation is more spontaneous, more natural."

"The more relaxed and calm I am, the more people hear me."

"I apply information to situations by sharing stories, examples and perspective."

"If I don't listen to them, I can't brag about them."

"I consciously think, who should get this information, who should hear it, understand it, and take action on the message I hear."

"If I feel my own face contorted, I can uncontort it with a shake of my head." (Nonverbal communication)

"Always talking mostly problems and issues with people promotes a problem-centric interaction and focus in the relationship, keeping it shallow." (This comment proved itself to be a frequent cause for leaders experiencing low relationships.)

"Communicate by saying, 'Save ten dollars or 20 percent of monthly or annual operating costs,' NOT just by saying, 'Help the client save expenses.' Just as we say goals should be specific, we as leaders can't stop there. For some of us, it does stop there. We also need to continue that degree of specificity in our daily conversations that supports the goal attainment, and still be empowering, not confining."

"Listen to understand, before listening to respond."

"Some people will put on blinders. An example is when they determine a request deadline is an arbitrary date and is not important. I'll explain the customer requested this date for a reason, and I would rather avoid having to go back to them on this. This is an example of helping people get to your vantage point."

"Changing our habitual response to hearing a bad news message from 'Oh no' to 'How fascinating, how remarkable,' triggers a creative urge, drawing people in and engaging them."

Repeat the last comment above to yourself. How does that message of one role model's experience and awareness resonate with you? Do you hear a voice within asking, "Are you kidding me?" Or does the voice from within say, "Let's think about that some more." Recall the visionary leader's story in the second chapter referring to environmental influence. That leader's role was tactical, operational and reactive in nature, yet he was marked a visionary role model. He saw strategic thinking as a part of, not apart from, his role. This last comment, while not belonging to that visionary leader, models a behavior change that illustrates the point of his story.

What's most critical?

When I asked one participant what he considered to be the most important aspect of leadership overall, he responded, "Communication, and specifically asking questions and listening." He related working for the CEO of a company in his previous role. One day, the participant watched as both management and union personnel walked into a room and sat across a long table opposite one another, talking within their own group, but shunning the other side.

"Marty, they were walking in like mortal enemies, and by the end of the day, they were walking out as if hand in hand with one another, talking, and making plans."

I asked, "How did that happen?"

"Well, from what I can figure, it was the CEO. He sat at the end of the table and, for most of the day, he asked questions and listened. He might ask one side something and say, 'I noticed you seem to have a lot of commitment in your tone of voice. Can you tell me what is behind your passion?' As people on the other side listened to their concern, they began to see how similar they were at a fundamental level. By day's end, it was like a transformation had occurred."

What follows is a template example of an organization's effort at communicating efficiently. This organization is spread out geographically among disparate manufacturing plants. They take advantage of a common voice mail system, and use a template of what is determined to be critical information. This enables the larger service organization to both anticipate potential service breakdowns and react more quickly by leveraging resources of the larger, dispersed team.

"System voice mail: This is _____(location, assembly center), date is____, time is ____, currently experiencing problem with system _____, affecting _____(human resources, paint shop, assembly plant). Problem started at ____, there are _____ lost (production) units."

Team orientation

Behaviors for promoting a team orientation include: developing mutual accountability among team members; promoting productive cooperation between teams; delegating; leveraging an assortment of skills and styles of diverse work teams to achieve results; and publicly rewarding the team. What the role model leaders said...

"I always start team meetings with celebrating."

"I'll talk with the quiet ones individually before the team meeting occurs. It's a good warming up process, increasing their comfort level. 'Has anyone given thought to this question?' The quiet ones will speak up."

"Collaborative—I'll try to involve all in the decision making."

"With my large group, I'll use analogies, tell them they're just like a football team. Not everybody's a quarterback or a linebacker. We put people into the roles they best play. I'll put others in front of the customer sometimes, not always me. I don't want the quarterback hiking the ball because he'll get clobbered, so instead of our best technical person presenting, let's get the best presenter to present. That technical person knows he is there, ready to back up."

"We've learned to be careful. In previous years, we would tweak a solution, and it worked.

Today, one tweak may temporarily work, but you can create consistency problems with other teams— engineering, support teams, etc. Tweaks today require engaging the broader team."

"I went from running the team meetings to the team runs the team meetings, similar to a high school student council model."

"It's being a buffer for my team, not passing on all the criticism; instead, just saying, 'Thanks for trying.' Everyone is trying to do a good job."

"It comes from my volunteerism (outside of work). My sensitivity to others' needs crosses over. The team lead's refusal or hesitancy to do something means a request for help. He either doesn't feel competent or sees others as better than him or her. I'll say, 'You're better than that,' will be brief, and set a positive expectation."

"It's getting people to forget they're getting beat up—do things to get their minds off the business. Use a team builder. For example, play hangman, and the first one who figures out the drawing on the board gets a treat, or leaves early. Take an interest in their careers and in them as people."

"Change *from* asking how to help others *to* asking for help from others. When people can just say, 'I don't know, I need help,' it so changes into a team atmosphere."

"Everybody has to contribute something. In baseball, a good shortstop may not be a good hitter, but will save you two runs a game. The first baseman is a powerful hitter. So, too, let the team play off each other. Tougher when you have 24/7 coverage (twenty four hours a day, seven days a week) and the person not strong is on call. But you can't get everybody to be everything. Playing to their strengths is the priority."

"A representative from each of the teams meets once a week, which promotes the larger team working together."

"If it's something we must do, present to the team as how can we benefit?"

"Even with my eighty-five people, I listen, take notes and relate back to them individually."

"Within our regimented, check-things-off environment, we meet weekly as a group and decide together. Purpose is a forum for people to vent, say what they want, and we review the work, tasks, projects, progress and metrics (measurement indicators)."

"A paradox of happiness is that happiness is elusive. If focused on doing something, (especially for someone, for the team, something of value), then happiness is experienced."

"Always ask, 'What would make this a good meeting for you?'"

"Going from twenty-two individual sites to one team, I initially promoted collaboration by having each account manager bring three issues to the meeting. I told them, 'Tell me what you need in two and one-half hours. If all of you each get to your second issue, great. Start with your top issue.' They immediately started working together as a team."

"I introduce perspective to the team. For example, I'll tell them to think about how we have meaning and significance, as a part of nature. Realize the squirrel has to have meaning. What are they doing? Collecting nuts (like advance checks) for the winter. It's their livelihood. Their work has meaning. Beavers are self-directed teams building a dam in their own way. The results are what count; each one does it differently. The geese are honking, cheering the front-runner on. The team communicates about us as a team in meaningful ways that I know my peers are not able to accomplish."

"I don't play to win as my focus. I've learned to play for the team first, do our best and then compete with myself. Did we put forth our best effort? Did we accomplish what we set out to do? Be competitive for the team first, myself second, not focused on me winning. Don't get too high when winning, nor too low when losing. Winning is broader than the scoreboard or scorecard. Without team cohesion, superstars alone won't keep it. Cohesion plays off one another, picks each of us up."

"They hear, 'If you fail, we all fail. Support one another. Sure, this time, he is on point.' You end up seeing less heroes, more team."

"We're not all cogs in a machine, so it's not, 'Put three more people on that.' I know my people well and play to their strengths and give them challenges to build on. However, I do NOT turn them into someone they are not."

"What message do you send new prospects to your team? Is it to join us and you'll get this (selfish), or is it to join us and here's what you are going to be a part of (selfless)?"

"*Familiarity breeds contempt* is a saying that becomes a wall. Yes, it applies at the bar scene. No, it does not apply when sharing humor, recognizing what is important to each person, achieving a balance (between work and personal) and sharing at the workplace. It's the rare exception of a person who tries to take advantage of that."

"Too often we over-define ourselves by our job, our role, what we do. We often waste energy on resentment and anger, having so raised the stakes as to our existence. I use the word waste, because there is nothing we can do about those things outside our control. People die soon after retiring due to over-defining themselves as their role. We need to define ourselves to a higher importance."

"Shouting and talking out of turn *less* in a meeting is a function of feeling *more* secure."

"Building alliances and building team is all about building relationships."

"First message I give them: 'As a team, here's what we are trying to do, and we depend on you to accomplish this.' Secondly, I pass on thank you notes, recognition, for reaching these objectives and I follow up with them."

"I verbally credit them publicly, in front of other leaders. I acknowledge their mannerisms, thoughtfulness, the way they helped so and so."

"I pair people together who typically bug one another, using a business reason to do so. The bugging always evaporates."

"I'll match new team members with a mentor/sponsor."

"To overcome organizational silos, I drive vendors and teams across different organizations to teleconference together. We deliver and communicate with one another. We ask, 'Who by name did you talk to?' Then we go to that person."

"I'm asking questions like, 'Who can do this, based on your experience?'"

"I developed an unstructured mentoring. It's a pairing of people with complementary strengths and weaknesses. The premise being people are more comfortable talking with peers than always being coached by their leader, and the team becomes stronger."

"After a team teleconference, I will call people individually and ask, 'What did you think of that?'"

"The belief behind my delegating is that people will always do more than you."

"Delegating enables occasional chats, or checkpoints, to coach, see how they are progressing, share ideas and appreciate."

"Help people work through it, don't do it for them."

"I'll openly discuss what each person is doing and his participation in the whole process. I'll stay loose, include a little humor and then ask, 'Any decision on what we need to do still remaining?'"

"Don't let people go empty-handed when they come asking for help. Do give them a name and phone number, because it takes courage for the person to come to others for help."

"The team always updates a missing member, and practices other interdependencies."

"When leading a team of leaders, it becomes even more paramount to give them space, accept their differences, than when leading individual performers."

One leader used a personal example describing how she promoted mutual accountability among team members. This simultaneously touched on time management, work-life balance, diversity, integrity, fairness and setting the example, within the broader function of people care.

As a busy manager, she scheduled her day by her priorities. When her child had a soccer game at 4 p.m. during a weekday, she would note soccer on her calendar. She indicated how important she felt that people not only heard the message, but also saw the message of work-life balance in practice. She effectively communicated that, when necessary, take some part of the workday to honor a personal issue. That became the expectation. And while some of us might think this would open the door to being taken advantage of, her feedback results showed just the opposite. She showed evidence of a high-producing team with high morale, mutual respect and accountability.

Diversity and team

It becomes obvious that leaders high in team orientation also have a sense for appreciating and acknowledging the differences and diversity among us, and using them to help make money in a business setting. Some of the following role model comments more closely illustrate this.

"I'll draw or you'll draw. I don't have a right way or a wrong way, I have a result."

"We changed from arguing all the time as a team to appreciating and valuing the differences among us. Diversity is about tradeoffs, and openly discussing."

"Perception becomes your projection."

"If you are afraid to learn, if you are not self-confident, then you are less inclined to work with others and help others."

"I get the relevant people together and regularly brainstorm, create the environment, give them the opportunity, mix them up. All this diversity equals a productive business as usual."

"Ask yourself what role do you provide—are you a pioneer, always pushing the edge? Or are you a settler, following in trace to settle, to develop, behind the pioneers?"

"Look at their calendar to see what's important to them. What do they most value, and what does their language indicate?"

"If it's a style approach, then I'll defer. If it's a material difference, then I'll ask questions."

Bonus—change

I noticed a few comments made by the role model leaders touching on change when reviewing this particular section, so I present a few of their thoughts as a bonus here.

"To cope and adapt to imposed change, I ask, 'What are the things out of my control? What are our abilities, competencies…are we really losing, or is it all surface noise?' I emphasize an aspiration-based mindset."

"Stormin,' Formin,' Normin'—we aren't able to get past the first two steps (Stormin' and Formin') to get people to see the results of their success, due in part to not leaving leaders in place long enough to see the consequences of their actions. For example, I've had five successive leaders in three years, while not changing my role. That is not productive change. We never get to our peak, to achieve what we set out to do."

"Circumstances change, yet happiness is a choice. For older people, lows are less low, because they accept things they can't change when older."

"I'm seen as a change agent because of my lifetime belief in Churchill's statement to move forward and never regress."

"I first consider the tradeoffs, then focus on implementing change."

"I'll hear, 'But it should be this way,' and I respond, 'No, that changed. Let's roll with the change, figure out how we build those relationships."

"People appreciate advance communications, especially in hard times. Present the context, here's the plan. Take change, for example. 'We're going to move this group from here to here. This is what is behind the move; these are the business reasons.' Usually people respond, 'Let's do it.'"

"Communicate, communicate, communicate. Communicate early wins; distribute a client's thank you letter. Things you find can communicate the turnaround; then the reengineering, or the change, are accomplished."

"People adjust to their situation, recover rather quickly."

"If we can't acknowledge we made a mistake, we can't change."

For me, one of the behavior changes that the role model leaders provided requires a change of language. Not a change from one national language to another, yet they have demonstrated to me a need to learn a new language. I can already speak the words, however, these words do not come natural to me, given years of speaking limited to one particular way. It is the language of asking questions in place of a lifetime of primarily making statements during certain, reoccurring conversational sequences, regardless of the topic. It does not mean that I only ask questions. What it does mean is that I balance my tendencies to declare statements with an appropriate tendency to enquire, seek clarification, sound and be curious, and appreciate what is external to me.

This chapter's quote

"Taking ourselves too seriously is a function of valuing the task. Taking ourselves or things less seriously is a function of valuing the relationship, more time with people." When I listened to the participant make that statement, I knew he was speaking to me. I had often heard feedback, offered throughout my life, that I took things seriously, or revealed a high level of sensitivity. Another habit of mine was to entirely focus first on getting the job done before I spent any time socializing or thinking of others. So while I was coaching this person, he, too, was coaching me. I have now reached an understanding of the limitation of my habit. When they say you can't change what you don't first acknowledge, this comment helped me take my first step—to acknowledge.

Have you possibly been coaching others and not even be aware you were?

We are closing in on the ultimate area—that being leadership. But first, what do the role models for high integrity and conviction say?

8

Integrity and Convictions

"I don't try to tell God what to do, I just report for duty."

- Participant

Listening to the role model leader make the comment above while discussing integrity, I realized a common thread among leaders of highest integrity. They share a gift of humility, of perspective, no matter what their title, accomplishment or education degree. They are guided by a continual sense for serving a higher meaning, a higher purpose. This goes beyond serving Wall Street expectations. This gives them courage to rise beyond the rules.

Questionable practices motivated by something less, by greed, have tainted the reputation of some of our leader stewards at the head of corporate America during the not too distant past, incurring a compromise of integrity. This exposure of illegal practices reminds us that integrity and values based on conviction should be, and is not always, a given among those trusted to oversee at the highest levels of our business organizations. However, the vast majority of senior and chief executives continue to reflect the highest standards of integrity. They just don't capture the news headlines for doing so!

125

The practices of stewardship and other best practices of leaders are rooted in integrity. Translated, this means that all the behaviors and statements you have read previously in this book mean nothing if done with an ulterior motive. It means little to sit next to people in conversation, or to ask a "what" question in place of a "why" question, or to be available and accessible as a coach, if your motive is other than honorable. Your motive should not be to pretend, to look good in front of others, or to be popular, as opposed to being authentic, connecting and learning. This illustrates the previous comment mentioned under creating a team orientation. "A paradox of happiness is that happiness is elusive. If focused on doing something, (especially for someone, for the team, something of value), then happiness is experienced."

Behaviors under integrity and convictions include: demonstrates honesty; builds trust; shows respect for others; keeps commitments; fosters ethical behavior; maintains courage and composure during hard times and difficulty; honors fairness in the workplace; and exhibits consistency in actions, decisions and words (walks their talk).

One of the earliest patterns of responses that surprised me came from leaders receiving an extreme of higher or significantly lower marks for demonstrating honesty. My intrigue began when one role model participant credited composure for such high markings for honesty. He cited maintaining calm, especially during periods of agitation, confusion and stress. Other subsequent role model leaders also referred to maintaining their demeanor. This surprised me, for I had not considered calm demeanor to be such a factor behind a perception of honesty.

Sharing feedback with one leader, he expressed shock as he noticed his lower markings for the honesty behavior. He sincerely saw himself as a person of honesty and integrity and could not initially believe this was his data, that this was the perception others had of him. He was raised believing in the importance of honesty and integrity. After some exploring, I asked him, "Do you see yourself as maintaining your cool, displaying a calm, composed demeanor when tensions run high, or do you raise your voice and show what others would see as visible anger or agitation?" After some conversation, it became evident this leader saw himself as a screamer. His habit was

126

to raise his voice, shout at people and display a high degree of excitability. I then asked him what kind of leader would he rather want to deliver bad news to, given a choice. Do you prefer to give news to a calm, self-controlled person, or one raising his voice and showing aggressive, nonverbal facial and body expressions? I asked him what was his sense when people faced the prospect of delivering bad news to him. Did they look forward to it?

"In anticipating your reaction," I asked him, "could some want to deliver only part of the message, or even avoid telling you the truth altogether? Did that make for even increased frustration later?" As we explored this further, other issues surfaced to bring about a bigger picture. What this leader realized was that his very reaction was creating the lack of integrity that others associated with him. Others were saying they could not be honest with him! He realized even his own family could not always feel safe to have an open, honest and frank conversation with him. He further raised the question of maturity that he was displaying. We had a very productive conversation, and you can be sure that this leader not only had an idea of how to behave differently, he was motivated by beliefs that were most important to him. I call this a life changing conversation.

This story continues

The pattern that followed maintained this track. That demeanor could be a primary player on the court of integrity and honesty became more understandable to me. Issues of truthfulness, questionable motive and character remain as factors for leaders perceived lower in honesty by others. However, time and time again, leaders seeking to understand a relatively lower perception of their honesty feedback, when asked if they maintained a consistent and fairly calm disposition on a regular basis, admitted to an inconsistent disposition. Inconsistent by expressing frustration and irritation ranging from a raising of the voice on one end of the spectrum, to outright screaming, usually laced with profanity, on the other end of the spectrum. Their culture and environment seemed to enable them, in their minds, to regularly behave in this way, yet feedback from others gave them low marks in honesty and respect. These leaders thought there were payoffs for this behavior that reinforced their belief in acting accordingly. The tangible and personal data in front of them, coming from people that mattered to them, and their willingness to think about it differently during our feedback conversations, made for much personal learning for me. After all, these leaders were also good people.

If there was an exception to this trend, it may come from the screamer who is not directing emotions at any one person, rather at the issues, and screaming encouragement. But experience presenting feedback indicates that to be just that—an exception, and exceptional indeed! I worked for one possible exception. More about him later.

Another surprise which keeps me curious

Over the course of five years of feedback coaching, I used a series of different versions of feedback, all covering broad areas of leadership. One of these versions had a behavior statement for demonstrating honesty immediately followed by a behavior statement for building trust. I was surprised to note a pattern of participants receiving high markings for honesty, yet simultaneously, significantly lower markings for trust. I say this surprises me, because I had always equated honesty and trust as close relatives, and if you earned the one, you had the other as well. Not always.

I thought the first time I encountered a leader high in honesty and trust, he would shed some light on the subject for me. I was not disappointed. A role model for both behaviors provided me a lead, a theory to work with. But it did not come easily at first.

You know how you ask someone for an opinion and they do not have one, but when you offer them your opinion, then it becomes a catalyst or thought-provoking idea? They suddenly have an opinion and tell you what they think. It happened here, as follows.

"I have noticed this trend of feedback for some leaders higher for honesty and lower for trust, and not the other way around. Do you have a thought as to how that can be?"

(Participant) "No, I don't know."

"Well, since the word 'quickly' is added to the trust behavior, I've been thinking it is connected to whether you are an extrovert or an introvert. As you know, extroverts more readily engage in conversation with others and maybe earn trust more quickly than the extreme introvert who tends to be quiet and not engaging as quickly."

With that, I could see this leader's expression suddenly change, and he replied, "Marty, this is not about personality preference, this is about philosophy. And my philosophy is, when I meet people for the first time, I trust them. And even if they do something wrong, it's not like I see them as intentionally getting up out of bed in the morning so they can make life miserable for themselves and others."

Over the course of a few hundred participants, using this version of feedback, when their feedback was significantly lower for trust than it was for honesty, I would ask them this question. "If you are aware of having a preference and can answer this question, when you meet people for the first time, is trust a given or do people first have to earn your trust?"

With rare exception, all participants with lower trust feedback answered that people had to earn their trust.

When I encountered the fewer participants marked as role model for both the honesty and the trust behavior and asked this same question, every one of them, to my honest recollection, replied that trust was initially a given. This, too, sounded like a broken record.

As a side note, the version of feedback I experienced for my own personal feedback (I, too, sat in the hot seat and had my feedback coach), had an honesty behavior, but it was not followed by a trust behavior. There was also a specific behavior that indicated whether people perceived you as manipulating situations for personal gain, which may get close to overlapping with trust. But that behavior statement did not specify trust. I would have been interested in how I was perceived for trust. After high school, I thought about becoming a priest and went to a seminary. I decided that was not for me and was able to enter the Naval Academy in Annapolis. In my senior year there, a billet I was assigned (midshipmen generally took on some student leadership billet as a senior within the brigade) was that of honor officer. I always supposed it was because they presumed anyone from a seminary background should be trusted to be the honor officer! As a Marine, I was assigned a military police occupational specialty. Because of that experience, I thought I had tended to be more one who believed people had to earn my trust, that trust was not a given. Hence, my interest in how I would have been perceived.

Business meaning and application

The significance of this discussion is that I noticed a strong association between the honesty and trust behaviors with behaviors in other categories. Take delegating, for example. Leaders who believed that others had to first earn their trust did more commonly receive lower frequency feedback for the delegating behavior. Here, again, it was the participant leaders making the connection to delegates and making that tie. They indicated that because people had to first earn their trust, it became noticeable in how they delegated what to whom. For some participants who indicated a tendency to micromanage, they were now able to tie it back, at least in part, to a personal philosophy or belief that they had developed over time around trust of others.

A few questions for you

Do people have to first earn your trust, or is trust given initially?

If people have to earn your trust, how might that affect the perception of others as to your being fair in the workplace?

How might that affect your relationships with various people in other ways?

How might that affect your ability to build teamwork, and a sense of team among disparate groups of people?

Could this limit your ability to resolve conflict?

Could this belief cause you to be seen as inconsistent between what you say (I'm delegating to you, which says I trust you) and what you do (I want to change the rules midstream, or I want to check your work, or I want to correct your work, or I want you to do it my way)?

Could your belief in people earning your trust cause you to behave or think in a way that actually influences others to respond such that their actions reinforce your belief that trust must be first earned?

What's your payoff for this belief?

What can you lose?

Are people (to include your children and any other people important to you) more confident or less confident as a result of your belief?

If people are less confident, how does that affect their commitment and stake in what you are collectively about as a work team or family unit?

Do you have a choice in this?

I cannot yet say that one philosophy is definitively better or worse than the other. They are both working philosophies. However, based on the patterns of perception and the corresponding insights and reflections of the participants involved, it is worth taking a closer look at both, and if your philosophy is either that people generally first have to earn your trust, or that trust is a given, now is a good time as any to revalidate it.

What follows again are some statements I collected from various role model participants for behaviors revealing integrity and courage of convictions. These include more comments on trust. Use these as a means for thinking about your own beliefs about integrity and convictions. How do your actions and words reflect your beliefs?

"Integrity is having a fine sense of one's obligation."

"I say, 'I screwed up' with the global team. People become more open, safe to admit shortcomings, and work towards development." (Trust)

"If people's philosophy is 'Trust must be earned,' it promotes a mentality that you must prove it, which immediately puts people on the defensive. You're looking to catch me in a lie, in a mistake."

"My composure comes from (1) recognizing things I can't control; (2) keeping a perspective;

compare this to a person being shot; and (3) when I feel the stress rising, I think pleasant memories, about the deer I bagged, or I go jog."

"I've learned to manage my anger. I become an observer of my anger. Temper is a typically destructive expression or response. Observing my anger encourages more of a constructive response and I feel physically less stressful. I try to understand what I'm feeling and why, because I find it's always more about me, less about them. They only trigger something in me that has nothing to do with them. I otherwise choose to let them trigger me, and live in personal confinement, or I can live in personal freedom. The choice is mine."

"High trust means I think before I talk, influencing their perceptions, and I role-play with them. It includes my tone of voice, body language and self-awareness. I might lower my voice, for emphasis. I'll ask questions like, 'What else do I need to do? What can I do for you? Do you understand the position I am in?'"

"I tend to think the best of people until they prove otherwise." (Trust)

"Don't underestimate people, and let them prioritize, make choices. You, as the leader, support and communicate changing priorities."

"As a leader, I hold myself to the same standards as my group. I do whatever I ask of them." (Trust)

"'OK, here's the dilemma, here's the situation. We can't control this. I'm with you, too, in the same boat. We're in this together.' This translates that they can relate, that I have genuine concern." (Respects)

"Trust, as a given up front, means proactive, means expecting the best. Requiring others to first earn your trust is reactive."

"When going home, I always think to myself, 'What else could I have done today to help?' This prompts ideas and possibilities for follow-up." (Respects)

"It includes my attentiveness to communicating face to face even more than expected with people who are remote." (Respects)

"It's acting on it, and seeing them, and not delaying…how can I help you be successful in your next job?" (Trust)

"It's a willingness to call yourself wrong." (Trust)

"It's looking more for the positives than the negatives in people. I look for what's under the appearance." (Trust)

"I never have to remember what I told you. I'm always telling the truth."

"What is said in here stays in here." (Trust)

"Trust is communicating the limitations of what I can and cannot do. It's admitting my mistakes, and having a constant dialogue about doing what's right."

"If they can get you riled up, you've lost. No matter how much they're fuming at you, if you show externally that you are affected or bothered, then you lose." (Maintaining composure)

"Trust is two factors. First, being proactive about people care, coaching, compensation and customer relations. Secondly, it's about being a servant steward leader."

"It's situational, because one can be honest about having gone behind one's back, such that honesty is high and trust is low."

"When I talk with my people, there are no interruptions, unless I'm paged, which requires immediate response." (Respects)

"People who don't relate well to each other can relate to me. I'll jump into frays. When mistakes are surfaced, I become all business, looking for issues, not feeling and blaming. Humor breaks the tension. My thinking is to get them to step back. 'There's issues on both sides. We're all sharing frustration. Let's move on to problem solving.'" (Trust)

"I ask in performance review, does anything surprise you? If substantially yes, we haven't done our job."

"I make the time." (Respects)

"Initially, with new people, I'll briefly explain, comment on a deep facial expression." (Trust)

"I tell people I do not want them NOT telling me something because they'll hurt my feelings." (Trust)

"I constantly address the rumor mill." (Trust)

"I care about you as a person first, as an employee second. I was raised in a 'show me' upbringing, with an action bias. If I can avoid red tape, procedural paperwork, I will." (Respects)

"I'll consciously slow my rate of speech, almost measured, talking slower than I'm thinking." (Respects) (This illustrates by example in chapter five on resolving conflict, the notion of increasing a space between impulses we experience and our reaction or response to these impulses.)

"I'll ask, 'Can you do this for us?' I get people involved. What makes me right is making you feel you're right." (Trust)

"I respond to personal requests on a timely basis...accessibility." (Respects)

"What I'm here for is for them. It's not to be the next, or even future, CEO (chief executive officer). What you see is what you get. If you don't like that, let's work through the issues. I can appear upset, but I never swear." (Respects)

"Fastest way to an untrustworthy organization is to not trust them."

"I talk face to face when possible, before calling them on the phone, because I am gone a lot (traveling). I put my people first." (Respects)

"I'm always open, give people the benefit of the doubt. An especially young team will assume the worst without the big picture." (Trust)

"I'll dismiss hearsay, get to the issues...ask, 'Is it founded?'"

"I'm very responsive to people in need, responsive to issues, questions, concerns. This is being both open and nonjudgmental."

"Communicating the big picture expands the boundaries of influence and impact that employees see they have from the customer service center to the management center. It creates a mindset." (Does this not increase the employees' potential for empowerment and for expanding their horizon of opportunity?)

"Here's who I am, what I'm looking for." (Trust)

"Each day, before I open the door, I remind myself to be part of the solution, and help them to solve, not become a part of the problem. Not find fault, blame and seek a victim or scapegoat. That's the job of a screamer. There is no success without a successor."

"I don't try to tell God what to do, I just report for duty."

"I listen, see the coachable moment, drop what I do, and show full interest." (Respects)

"I listen with patience. I have regular one-on-ones, not sudden one-on-ones." (Walks the talk) (This participant leader critiques a common practice by some managers and leaders to suddenly hold one-on-one meetings with their employees as a leadership intervention in reaction to some perceived need.

Instead, this leader maintains that those one-on-ones are a constant practice, not a temporary fix to address some morale issue that surfaced on a recent employee survey.)

"Say what you mean, mean what you say."

"I can't always say yes, because there is trust." (Keeps commitments) (This participant maintains that if she were to always say yes, eventually she would not meet other commitments already made, and violate trust over time.)

"There is an assumption that if you say no, you are not a team player. You must see 'no,' as an occasional priority, can still say things like, 'Here's who you call.'"

"Our 'busyness' is often our excuse to avoid embarrassment."

"By providing encouragement, and let them fumble. They are going to if they are really into the game."

"Being calm means I believe that there is a solution to everything. I don't point fingers, which creates conflict. Fix the problem, not the person. The person already knows!"

"It's being matter of fact." (Honesty)

"One needs to be genuine, but not brutally honest. It's the difference between saying, 'No thanks. I don't want to,' and saying, 'I would never go out with the likes of you!'"

"I don't say, 'Don't tell people this.'" (Trust)

"It's treating everyone as equals, not treating everyone equally. Treat the situation, where they are at (in their life)."

"Apologizing is the very act of admitting concern for fairness."

"I'll say no, even if they don't like it." (Ethical)

"I'm consistent in how I treat people."

"Do you often think, 'What will go wrong,' or do you more often think, 'What will go right?'" (On generating high self-confidence and calm demeanor)

"If I focus on what's wrong, or could be wrong, I become a worry hog. That's toxic. The remedy is to walk around, take a few deep breaths, splash cold water on my face, pray and meditate. It's a spectrum from no worry, which is denial, to toxic worry, which is whatever can or will go wrong, does. In the middle of the spectrum is normal worry, good worry, where I find I am anticipating, looking forward to the moment of taking action."

"Keep your expectations, but be willing to accept less." (When the participant stated this, I replied that I came from a Marine Corps culture where you 'inspect what you expect,' and asked him to clarify his meaning. He then replied, "I mean, unless you taught them, don't assume they already know.")

"I lower my voice to calm the person in tears."

"Spite and resentment is like taking a poison and expecting someone else to die."

"Reacting with emotion gets you in trouble. Sit back, pause, then act."

"I might second guess your reasoning, and your way of arriving at a conclusion, but I do not second guess your confidence, or who you are."

"Respect is the golden rule. I don't take things personally, I do not hold grudges, and I care about them. No matter what I'm doing, when my door is open and you come in, I turn to greet you. I'll drop what I do and show my full interest."

"With my New York accent, my timing and speech is different from the mid-westerners here, so I'm looking for a pause, when to jump in." (Respects)

"I'll slow down, think slower, and put off immediate decisions until I am calmer."

"For the last eight years, my career decisions have been guided by the belief that when I shy away from an opportunity, and it is because I feel too guilty, then I am taking too much on. When I shy away from an opportunity, and it is because I am afraid or uncomfortable, then it's the opportunity I should take."

"Respect, confidence and trust are three fingers to the same hand you deal others."

"Doing the right thing for the right reason is usually harder in the short term, but living with the consequences of that right reason is usually easier in the long run."

"People look for integrity, so (1) admit your mistakes, they look for you owning it; and (2) continually keep their focus, like saying, 'Guys, this is coming. The boss is not aware of it yet; how can I help you be ready?' Anticipate their questions. 'I won't bring it to the boss' attention this week, guys, but by next week, tell me what you're doing.'"

One of the comments from a participant above which stated, "Say what you mean, mean what you say," can be practiced by again raising an idea in the chapter on resolving conflict. As you recall, the intent was to increase a space between the impulses we encounter and our response or reaction to those impulses. One of the techniques offered was to ask yourself a question like, "What is it I most want to say right now?" By hearing yourself even respond with, "What I most want to say is...," we may find our conversation more typically reflects saying what we mean and meaning what we say. This is one helpful way to increase maintaining a consistency between what we say and do, between our attitudes and behaviors.

On becoming unstuck

I listened to one speaker relate a story that she had experienced. The point of this story gives one method for helping people think about how to maintain a more level demeanor when the stress is rising. This can also be used to help discover the visionary, the creative, within each of us. This presents an alternative when feeling stuck—stuck by habits of the past, or stuck by an inability to think one's self out from a vicious cycle. The story goes like this. A martial arts master in aikido placed a hold on a student and instructed her to break out of the hold. After some frustration on the part of the student, the master released the hold and coached the student. In essence, he asked her what she had been thinking the whole time she was attempting to break the hold.

The student replied, "I can't move this arm. I tried and can't move that."

The master said, "So where was your mind focused?"

The student's reply, "On where I was stuck."

"Where else could your mind be focused?" asked the master.

"On where I am not stuck?"

"Yes. Focus your mind on where you are free to move."

So the master reapplied the hold, without any less degree of difficulty from the first time. The student started thinking to herself, "Well, I can move my fingers, my left elbow shifts slightly to the right, my one foot moves, my head goes this way."

In a matter of a few short minutes, the student had freed herself from the hold.

Just as the student experienced, we can turn our frustration into satisfaction, failure into success, and our lack of motion into motion, by first recognizing our thought patterns. As the student did, we can consciously shift a thought pattern from one focused on being stuck, on what we can't do or can't move, to one focused on being unstuck, on what we can do and are free to move. Did you already note that the master coached in terms of the positive, what to do?

Once you determine a particular behavior pattern is ineffective, you will discover ways to replace the old behavior pattern with a new behavior pattern. Some would say that it starts with a new way of thinking. And I would say that a new way of thinking starts with a new awareness to what we did not realize previously, or to what we did not realize the full extent of previously.

Many consider integrity to be the basis for leadership, our next chapter.

9

Leadership

*"What did the monkey say when they cut off his tail?
'It won't be long now!'" - Joe Schips*

There was an old German, Joe, who owned a nursery and garden center east of Cincinnati. He had fought on Germany's side in World War I, then came over to America before the start of the Second World War, and remained. He and his wife had no children, and he always employed a young helper to assist him with the business. His last helper had just been drafted into the Army and he had a vacancy. It was here that I entered the picture and started working at my first job ever.

Joe's property stretched back for several acres from the main road. On it, he had two ponds and stretches of trees and other plants, which he grew and maintained. My first day on the job, he taught me how to drive the tractor. It was an old farm tractor, the type you started by rotating a lever, or cranking, from the front of the tractor. Still, on that first day, he had me hook a trailer to the tractor and drive towards the rear of his property. There, he showed me how to dig out a tree and burlap the base of it. There were some other plants to be dug, and later he returned to see how I had done.

143

Having placed the plants on the trailer, I was to drive them to the front, where a customer who had selected them earlier would arrive to purchase and pick up the order.

Being the novice tractor driver that I was, and having not as yet developed my decisiveness, I was faced with a choice as to which way to maneuver around the ponds on my return. Do I follow to the side of both of them, or cut between the two ponds and go on around? As I changed my mind and made a split-second decision to go between the ponds, I turned the wheels. The front wheels had entered the shoulder of one pond and started to head down the gradual slope. In an instant, I recalled being certain in my mind to stop the tractor by depressing the clutch pedal. To my dismay, I continued down the proverbial slippery slope into the pond. I had forgotten about the two handles on either side of the seat, *called brakes*, designed to stop each of the two bigger rear wheels.

There I sat, with water up to my chest and just the vertical tail pipe protruding from the water's surface in front of me. Joe, who maintained a visual and watched what happened, was a huge, temperamental German. He was known, as I learned later, to raise his voice and talk in German. However, on this occasion, he came running around the pond, splashed in, and was only concerned that I was alright. There I still sat, my hands gripping the steering wheel.

As it turned out, Joe called the farmer next door, who came over with his tractor and a chain and pulled out the tractor I had dunked. It took Joe a week before he was able to get the tractor to run again. He continually repeated a process of draining and drying.

I happened to be at work when Joe turned the tractor over for the first time, successfully starting it. As soon as that had occurred, he turned to me and said, "Here she is."

Not once had Joe raised his voice in anger and told me what I should or should not have done. Yes, he had coached me again about the use and function of the brake handles, as I exclaimed that the clutch did not bring the tractor to a stop like I had been told! And now, to my complete surprise, he was inviting me to get back on the tractor, in a voice that sounded totally certain and not the least bit tentative. He was inviting me to get on, even before himself, the very man who had diligently worked to fix it. As I lifted myself onto the seat, I remember that sense of relief that something bad that I had caused was now made to be OK. And I was more than just determined to not repeat my mistake. I was determined to get to work.

For the four years that I worked for Joe, whenever he raised his voice, I never sensed that it was directed at me. Besides, he would eventually and regularly boast to customers that I was the best worker of all the hired help he had employed through all the years. And, on occasion, when a fun moment was needed, Joe would make a reference to the tractor in the pond incident.

There is a question that has periodically visited my mind through life. It's the old chicken and the egg story—which happened first? Did Joe's labeling me as the best worker that he had ever had begin with the way he handled my major error on day one and week one, an error that directly impacted his livelihood, at least temporarily? After all, a tractor was a major part of his business, and he had no backup.

Did Joe come across as a manager or as a leader? I have often smiled to myself whenever I heard any debate around what is leadership and how does it differ from management. Some refer to the science of management and the art of leadership, as one distinction between the two. I like this description, even though it is limited. On day one, and on week one, of my employment career, I saw both leadership and management, and I saw how they worked together. I experienced leadership as reflecting the power and grace of what it means to be human. For sure, the difference for me was not the management that Joe exercised on that first day and week in recovery and maintenance. The difference was his leadership. Any number of people could have practiced the management that Joe exhibited so well. However, it took the best that is in each of us, which surfaced in Joe so clearly that first week, to enable me to experience leadership so vividly early on.

So which occurred first, my being Joe's best worker or Joe's humanity and leadership? It is in recognition of the power of Joe's character, shown through example and through his composure under fire, that I recognize what Joe's leadership did for me. It enabled any potential I had for accomplishing and learning to emerge and be realized. It was my potential that the leadership I experienced called forth. It was leadership turning an unproven laborer into a proven laborer, turning a new chapter in my life's experience, which management alone could not do. It brought out the best in me.

Another example of Joe's leadership occurred a few years into my working for him. He had always wanted to return to his hometown and visit relatives he had not seen for many years. Since I had developed a handle on the business, and relationships with many of his customers, Joe and his wife left me in charge of the business for a week. During that time, some old friends they had known for years would bring the money in when I opened the shop. They would return that early evening when I closed the shop and take the days' proceedings. Can you imagine what it was like for this high school student to experience the responsibility and joy of maintaining a business, making customers happy, and offering them advice, and with no supervision? I was it. Would a person focused on managing entrust their livelihood like that? No, that scenario would have been managed differently. Again, the difference here was leadership.

Maybe I was just fortunate to have experienced something so dramatic and memorable as my first day, and first week ever, working. I witnessed my first personal look at leadership in a business setting.

We have been talking leadership since page one of this book. The comments that follow are some I captured from role models when talking specifically about leadership. Some of these comments could have appeared in previous sections. Which ones speak to you?

"Constant short-term reaction means always changing our words, which means contradictions, because people can see the short term over the long term."

"Clearly articulate values, what's important, which is articulating the long term, the big picture."

"Learning is not trying to do it all myself, and letting go."

"If you don't meet your employee's priority, they won't meet yours. Provide the environment in which they want to be motivated."

"Managing is analogous to controlling the snow. You can build a huge building to block its path, or put out a little snow fence and some pieces of wood, so the snow will drift that way."

"I emphasize perspective versus all-knowing. I position my people with the different clients, and tell them not to report back to me every contact, just significant information and highlights."

"One distinction between a leader and a manager is this. If you have one leader, they should set and communicate the strategy such that their 200 managers implement the vision and make necessary changes to ensure accomplishment. If no leader, you have 200 different visions and strategies."

"You can't do it all alone and you can't know it all alone. You must collaborate."

"Ask yourself what you want and need as an employee, and give that back."

"Three things: First, clearly state the expectations, what to accomplish; they should know what it takes for them to succeed. Not in the manager's way of thinking or doing, but in terms of the organization's objectives to be realized. Second, ensure you have time to give them feedback, and feedback on how the organization is doing. Also, give time to receiving feedback, to listening, to understanding what's being said (you don't have to agree). Third, reward and recognize. Nine out of ten times, recognition is more motivating than money.

Employees need to grow, reach their potential in responsibility, and grow in place."

Making mistakes is part of learning. Identify, appreciate and understand what your people most need."

"Do you see yourself as a director or as a leader?"

"It's like giving people different hats to wear when you are questioning them. If you sat in the boardroom meeting, would you do it differently?"

"People in Europe, the Middle East and Asia would give me feedback as such: 'I'm always laughing, smiling, always up,' so they say they feel at ease. I'm here to help, not be difficult. I surprise them by telling them things they wouldn't expect from me, like, 'I don't like this anymore than you do. I'll try to change this,' or 'Send me your thoughts. We'll try to change it.'"

"My personal style of leadership is to be on the fly, to be more effective, early on with a new team. Until they get to know you, a one-on-one meeting appears as more organized, less caring."

"Delegating is important to building a cultural organization of high performers. Delegating is not losing control, and delegating authority does not abdicate control. Have a good team, and turn them loose."

"Leadership development occurs on the job. Even through extended leader team meetings we role-play, do Q&A (question and answer sessions), and coach. Sam wants tuition reimbursement, what do we do? Our client just told us they will cut back, and Jan comes in and asks about her next raise. What do I say?" (The names used here are fictitious.)

"No one person is good enough to govern another without the other's consent."

"Examples of maintaining composure are sharing my stories, who I am, what I am about, staying positive, focusing on the end goal and result, looking through a storm of activity and helping people to focus."

"Behave like a leader, NOT like a boss. Be open and respectful to others' ideas and experiences. You go away from establishing the answers towards establishing the direction."

"When cash is not available, tell a person to take the day off with their family, if you know that is important to them. Tell their spouse, 'We're trying to make up for all that extra overtime in the past.'" (On the use of compensatory time)

"Positive and happy means you are focused on solutions. Negative and unhappy means you are focused on complaining."

"I work with my leaders to help them be the leader I want to work for. Your best job is working to understand who you are. Teach them to ask for help."

"Asking questions means involving them, which is NOT the autocratic leadership style." (On leadership style)

"Ninety-five percent of coaching is spontaneous, informal communications. It's less the formality."

"A leader is someone who helps you get somewhere you can't get to on your own."

"I see my effectiveness as a leader as seeing myself being like a pastor, practicing stewardship with my people."

"People won't know how good I am until we hit a problem together."

"The perception of me as a role model for development stems from usually small segments of three to four minutes, informal coaching conversations, not the formal, one-on-one meetings."

"When delegating to a new person, I just leave the deadline open-ended and see if they ask, 'When is it due?' Will they provide me some feedback and updates? If not, I will then set deadlines and clarify."

"I always push and encourage them in results, expectations, ownership, accountability and empowerment. 'What can you do about it?' They come to me after the fact; they'll say, 'This is the problem. I did that,' and I respond, 'Great! Think about this.'"

"Coaching is about time, availability. My premise for coaching is making myself available. I'm only as good as the people around me, versus the premise that I'm a star. It's easier to sabotage a star, harder to sabotage a team."

Some final stories

A participant once asked me if there was a single characteristic or quality from all the things that role models said they do which seemed to be most important.

In response, I told him that initially I would have said integrity, based on my personal experience previous to becoming a feedback coach. However, as a feedback coach, another common denominator that I heard from the role models was the ability to ask questions of others. This does not arise out of self-indulgence, nor is it narrow-focused. Rather, this seems to come from a mentality that spoke courage to those afraid to learn, caring to those who thought no one really cared, broader thinking to those who thought narrowly-focused, and engaging to those who felt uninvolved. Certainly, integrity remains a key factor. Indeed, one example of questionable integrity may lie in the people who are always asking questions that they think they already know the answer to, a form of manipulation that is not in the spirit of questioning that I hear coming from the role models. Unless they are specifically teaching, playing devil's advocate, or some like purpose that requires asking questions with preordained answers, instead the role models ask questions from a position of curiosity, and wanting to genuinely learn what the other person is thinking, and mutually benefit from the ensuing exchange.

There was another participant who was marked a role model by her respondents for promoting productive debate and discussion. She was an expert in her industry, and in her field, without question. When I asked her, 'What do you think you do or say…,' she replied that she always asks questions of others, particularly in meetings.

I then challenged her and said, "Surely you go into those meetings already knowing what the answers to problems are ahead of time, don't you?"

She replied in a humble kind of tone, "Yes."

"Then what makes you ask questions and take the time when you already have a good idea what the solution should be?"

She replied, "Marty, I am always curious as to what the others are thinking, and as I listen to them, I am always amazed at their thinking, their ideas, their perspective. I am then sharing my perspective as it relates to theirs, and often, I come to some different place, even a totally different solution, by the time we are finished. We are all the better for it."

This next story also reflects curious and open thinking. There was one leader participant who had people and clients spread around the world. During our introduction, he shared with me the multitude of problems that he faces. Having drawn from a wide cross section of diverse people from among his respondents, he was one of those people who had high marks across all the behaviors, among all the areas, which was exceptional to achieve. After all, some might be seen as role models in "people care," and less frequent in "risk taking" and "decisiveness." Some, again, might be high "integrity," yet low in the "business" and "visionary" areas, and so forth. This participant was high frequency across all the behaviors.

At one point, I asked him, "Is there one thing that you think you do which causes everybody to perceive you so high across all these behavior statements?" He thought for a few seconds, then said, "Marty, there is one thing I always do, whether I'm with one of my people talking their career, or with a client, especially a new client. I'm always asking these two questions: 'What is it you most want to have happen (during this meeting)?' Or, as an example, 'What would you like to most see happen during the next forty-five minutes that we are going to be talking your career?' The second question I'm always asking as a follow-up to the first question is, 'How can I support you?' or, 'What would you like from me?' I am always asking those two kinds of questions."

I learned the importance of asking, "How can I support you?" **after** having asked, "What is it you most want to have happen?" If I asked others how I could support them **before** they knew what they most wanted to have happen, their answer would more likely be futile.

Reflection

So how do the various ideas, practices, and beliefs embedded in the comments of the multitude of role model business leaders, speak to you?

What do you see as reinforcing what you already do?

What do you see as something you do or say, but only on rare occasion, that you could definitely leverage more often?

Which new behaviors or ideas could you see yourself doing and still be who you are?

In what ways could you measure your progress over an initial month, or longer period of time?

Which ideas and practices apply beyond the domain of work, to include relationships with others at home or school? Which apply while with neighbors and friends, or in any social setting, or while doing volunteer work?

Which practices could you modify to adapt to your situation, or to adapt to the needs of those you relate to?

If there is one idea that can cause you to turn what has been a breakdown into a breakthrough, then it is worth the price of this book and the associated time to read it.

Wrap up

I have one final story to wrap up, as an answer to what I think all these comments and ideas are saying and speaking to the reader.

There was an author and leadership philosopher, a wonderful man I have met named Peter Koestenbaum. He used to coach business leaders on leadership and transformation.

The very first time I saw him, he asked a number of leaders in a meeting, "What's your definition of leadership?"

We gave him a sampling of our best responses and I remember thinking that it just would not be on the same level that he was thinking. Our basic response was, "...the ability to influence people to act."

He responded by saying that he was still learning about leadership and, from his experiences and travels, he surmised leadership to be, "the ability to connect with another human being."

As I thought about his definition the following hours and days, I focused on the difference between the words "influence" and "connect." I realized that while the ability to influence people to act has merit (after all, I learned it in the military), to use that as my operating definition may lead me down a path to manipulate, coerce

153

or otherwise behave as a leader that may not be as productive as Peter Koestenbaum's definition. To connect with another human being speaks of power and humility. Peter would encourage you to think about coming from a position of authenticity as a person to accomplish this.

The theme of responses from the role model leaders speaks to me of connecting with other human beings. My interpretation of "other human beings" means that I see people first as human beings before I see them through the lens of some label—peer, direct employee, boss, vice president, maintenance worker. Influencing people to act, however, by the very words, can lead me to acting as if I'm on a stage, pretending, and take me away from authenticity.

Somehow, the people who are connecting have made it their business to know the subtle difference between asking a "why" question and a "what" question. They know to ask alternative questions, such as asking, "How can I motivate others," to alternatively asking, "What are the things I typically do or say, or the thoughts I think before doing them, that prevent others from feeling motivated?" These people are connecting by saying thanks in little ways over time, and by coaching in a spontaneous conversation as they walk a few short seconds with a person amid a busy, activity-filled day.

If you did not notice from those earlier examples, the world of role models is nonlinear. They understand that when they offer a quick "attaboy," they could be simultaneously coaching. Recall the employee receiving feedback from their leader as they leave a meeting together? The leader says, "I, for one, appreciate your biting your tongue in there for the last half-hour, and I know practicing patience is tough for you. But I think we all benefited from hearing the customer being able to vent." That employee receiving the feedback has also just been coached.

How are you connecting with other human beings, in little ways, every day? The opportunities continue to present themselves.

Joe retired from the garden center business shortly after I moved on and, some years later, I received news that he had died. Traveling to get to the funeral, I arrived just in time to make a request. I felt obliged to say a few words and, before the service began, asked the pastor if I could do so at some point during the service. While seemingly surprised to hear such a request, he asked Joe's wife, Rose. She said, "Of course." I experienced the privilege of speaking to the people to whom Joe meant so much. I included in the eulogy Joe's handling of the tractor in the pond. This became a universal life moment to share. All thanks to that thing called leadership, which happened to surface in Joe on an ordinary day in the early spring of 1969.

And about that quote that introduced our chapter on leadership. "What did the monkey say when they cut off its tail? 'It won't be long now.'" Joe would repeat that joke a few times to me over the years and he would chuckle each time. I noticed he would especially cite it as a tension breaker. I now cite it as the lead quote for our chapter on leadership. Quotes do not always have to be deep to be significant. It may sound out of place, but in reality, it is very much in its place. It's connecting with other human beings.

10

Conclusion

Many reasons exist for producing this book. One of my motives began with a statement made to me by a participant at the conclusion of his feedback. He made a revelation to me that he had kept private from our conversation.

"I have ADD (Attention Deficit Disorder), and have never sat for three hours like this before in my life until now, with you."

This one comment reflects the power of genuine feedback conversations I repeatedly experienced with people, for the sake of learning and seeking a more meaningful life.

This power cannot be captured in these pages. However, a glimpse into the learning can be, and it is my sincere hope, that it is the learning and discovery that helps clarify for you the meaning of life you seek to express and manifest through your behaviors.

What do you most want to be remembered for? Are you creating the legacy to which you aspire?

Go leave your mark, and have others be in your presence!

Appendix—Sample Comments and Questions from Role Models

"When writing music, something in my life is resonating; I just need to get out of the way, allow that to happen. It is very humbling."

"From the day you are born until you ride a hearse, nothing in between is so bad it could be worse."

"When you are focused on your own difficulty, you lose perspective, become self-absorbed. For example, the train lost an engine. Good news. You could be on an airplane!"

"There's a lot out there to be done that will get done, if you don't worry about who gets all the credit, about who gets there first."

"He who is convinced against his will is of the same opinion still; meaning, you can't browbeat them into another view, you must lead them there by asking questions."

"You tend to draw on positive past experiences, not on negative experiences."

"To the question, 'How do you live such a long life?' The simple answer, 'Just don't think about it.'"

"We can be as servants to our dreams, live through our imaginations, inspired by our vision of the future."

"There is no responsibility without knowledge."

"Where there is pain, there is opportunity."

"'Just because I am boss, 'my ideas go' no longer flies when replacing the hierarchy of position with the hierarchy of ideas."

"The hard question gets you the hard evidence."

"Rising tide lifts all boats."

"I just can't stay in this day alone. I am always six months out."

"In the difficult times, I'm there in their corner. When something is screwed up, I take the fall. I don't filter the venom down, only the learning."

"Life is about deciding. You never have all the data. That's life."

"Political is urgency based on 'whom' versus 'what.'"

"Risks, and promoting healthy risk taking, are simply being willing to let people see what you don't know."

"The higher up in leadership, the less of an employee you are to your leader."

"Measurement and litigation is making us default to certifications for excellence."

"I don't make a wrong decision. I make a decision based on the limited data and view I had. No need for guilt, you can relax about having to be right."

"Employees break things, and fix them. Leaders break trust and respect, which are slow and difficult to fix."

"I learn more by MBWA (Management By Walking Around) than through 300 e-mails."

"I used to be a flamer, until I discovered I lost not once, but twice, every time. Internally, I lost physically. Externally, they didn't hear my message."

"People don't care how much you know, until they know how much you care."

"Excuses only satisfy those who make them."

"To love is to seek to release the other."

"The difference between using the label 'weird' and the label 'eccentric' is, do I expect the worst in people, or the best in people?"

"Thought leads to an action, action to a habit, and habit to a character."

"Is your view of approaching your leaders with a problem as, 'I've failed?' If so, could that premise somehow be communicated to your employees as well, given their relationship to you as their leader?"

"Just like getting rid of clutter, removing activities and things that serve no purpose in our lives opens us up to more."

"Nothing can happen today that God and I can't handle."

"Not everybody can be famous, but everybody can be great. Greatness is determined by service."

"You can say they are high-maintenance employees who need babying, or you can say they are extra-sensitive employees who need understanding."

"Prejudging questions tend to be 'why' questions."

"We can do this better than either of us alone."

"It's the company's office, not my office. We are stewards."

"Can you be a good father, or a good executive, without doing this (coaching)?"

"How do you sell business if you develop trust only sometimes?"

"Getting things wrong is the price you pay for getting things done. Forget the mistake, remember the lesson."

"When two people on a team always agree, one of them is unnecessary."

"Life is too short to dwell." (On developing patience and listening)

"If I don't listen to them, I can't brag about them."

"What you resist persists."

"There is no such thing as a problem without a gift for you in its hand. I seek problems because I need their gift."

"When I am focused outward, it's always on them, it, other people, an issue out there. When I'm focused inward, it's about what I did, thought or said that affected other people, other issues."

"What choice presents the least amount of risk?"

"It's a lot easier to ignore a statement than to ignore a question."

"Those who don't make mistakes usually work for those who do."

"The best way to cope with change is to help create it."

"Do you just bitch, moan and groan, or also say, 'OK, now what are we going to do about it?'"

"What's your philosophy at work?" (Business is business, bottom line focused, all work and no play?)

"What do you want your legacy of leadership to be?"

"Am I still wearing the last bad experience on my face?"

"Sitting next to people, at an angle, prevents distractions from distracting."

"Brainstorming anticipates change."

"I would never ask, 'Why?' if I truly wanted to hear what they're trying to say."

"'Why,' 'but,' and 'so' are pillars of closed-mindedness."

"To the continued, 'Yes, but…,' I'll say, 'OK, if *that* were absent, what would you do?'"

"Either procrastination or focusing on little things first are the opposites of acting on vision and risk taking. The little things will always keep coming, keeping you otherwise preoccupied."

"A person cannot take on all that they possibly can, unless they take on more than they can possibly achieve."

"It's how one is **after** the conflict."

"Making fewer rules and allow more mistakes. A breakthrough was never inspired through rule books, which invite rigidity."

"Important thing about a loss is to not lose the lesson. Remember the lesson."

"You cannot dictate a solution to a conflict."

"Always leave something positive with the customer. A new insight, an interesting article, leave something with them."

"You can visit Pity City, you just can't move there."

"You show an interest in people, they'll work for you."

"The word 'why' sounds accusatory."

"Asking 'Why?' implies doubting, questioning in disbelief."

"If I feel my own face contorted, I can un-contort it with a shake of my head."

"...Don't get too high when winning, nor too low when losing. Winning is broader than the scoreboard or scorecard."

"Apologizing is the very act of admitting concern for fairness."

"It's treating everyone as equals, not treating everyone equally."

"Treat the situation, where they are at (in their life)."

"Do you often think, 'What will go wrong?' Or do you often think, 'What will go right?'" (On generating high self-confidence, calm demeanor)

"Changing our habitual response to hearing a bad news message from, 'Oh no' to, 'How fascinating, how remarkable' triggers a creative urge, drawing people in and engaging them."

"A paradox of happiness is that happiness is elusive. If focused on doing something (especially for someone, for the team, something of value), then happiness is experienced."

"Doing the right thing for the right reason is usually harder in the short term, but living with the consequences of that right reason is usually easier in the long run."

"When sitting next to people, I'm more relaxed and tend to let my guard down, which means I tend to let go of my prejudices and biases enough to hear most clearly."

"When positive and happy, I notice people are focused on solutions. When negative and unhappy, they're focused on complaining."

References

Fritz, Robert. *The Path of Least Resistance.* New York: Fawcett Columbine, 1984, pp. 68-70.

Marshall, Lisa J. & Freedman, Lucy D. *Smart Work.* Dubuque, Iowa: Kendall/Hunt Publishing Company, 1995, pp. 76-77.

Printed in the United States
17566LVS00007B/1-81